Jay R. Leach

Behold the Man

Satan's Secret Weapon Today: Ignorance of Truth

iUniverse, Inc.
Bloomington

iUniverse books may be ordered through booksellers or by contacting:

iUniverse
1663 Liberty Drive
Bloomington, IN 47403
www.iuniverse.com
1-800-Authors (1-800-288-4677)

ISBN: 978-1-4502-9286-3 (sc)
ISBN: 978-1-4502-9287-0 (ebook)

Printed in the United States of America

iUniverse rev. date: 04/26/2011

ACKNOWLEDGMENTS

To the students of the Bread of Life Bible Institute and to the pastors, ministers and disciples of the Bread of Life Church & Ministry Fellowship, whose willingness to take risks, accept innovation, and follow the Holy Spirit in planting churches and ministries to the glory of God.

To the disciples of our flagship, the Bread of Life Christian Center and Church, Whiteville, N.C. for their faith, teachable spirits, and ability to accept change in order to remain relevant in ministry.

To the churches to whom God has privileged my wife and me to be a part of through the pastorate over the past 28 years, we thank you. June 6, 2010, marked the end of our commitment in the local pastorate. Many of the principles expounded upon in this book were birthed out of our relationship with the local church in both small and large venues in multi-cultural and multiracial experiences. We now rededicate ourselves to God as disciple-making servants on the national and international level helping to restore and energize Spirit-filled old wineskins into new wineskins. It is the task of these new wineskins to pour out the new wine into this generation by passing on the revelation of God's truths through the witness of the Word and godly example.

The many, many saints in the Lord's service around the world serving as able apostles, prophets, evangelists, disciple-making pastors, teachers, and missionaries who acknowledge us as their spiritual parents in the Lord, we humbly and prayerfully commit to God. Their humble spirits, biblical worldviews, methods, kingdom attitudes and godly focus make them assets to the furtherance of God's kingdom purposes in these post-modern days.

To our children, grand and great grandchildren, whose tender and teachable spirits have allowed us to see and experience the third and fourth generation good seed; as they continuously plant the truth of God's Word into each new born. We praise God!

Jay R. and Magdalene J. Leach (2011)
Bread of Life Ministries International
Visit us at: www.breadoflifenc.com

All Scripture is taken from the New King James Version of the Holy Bible, except where noted.

INTRODUCTION

A study of the crucifixion of Jesus Christ reveals all of the great doctrines of the Bible: The deity of Christ, human depravity, our Lord's sinless life and work of atonement as a man, our salvation by grace through faith, the doctrine of reconciliation, the ministry of the Holy Spirit, Christ's second coming and so very much more. It is no wonder Satan is striving so hard to distract the body of Christ from its purpose and get any references and symbols of Christ and Christianity removed from the public square. What is so very sad is the fact that much of the church has seemingly fallen for this web of deception, by keeping Christ within the four walls and to one's own person. Satan accomplishes this through disrupting public knowledge of Jesus Christ; and he puts forth special effort to distract the body of Christ from the truth of God's Word.

The crucifixion of Jesus Christ is the very center of the Christian gospel and the Christian life. Not the birth, not the mighty miracles, not the sinless life of Jesus, but His death on the cross is the focal point of divine revelation. We must join the apostle Paul and state boldly, "God forbid that I should glory, save in the cross of our Lord Jesus Christ." How the apostle Paul properly defined the Gospel, Jesus Christ as a Man died for our sins on the cross; He was buried and He bodily arose from the grave on the third day according to the Scriptures. That is the Gospel of our

Lord and Savior, Jesus Christ and it is absolutely the essential and only true foundation upon which our reconciliation with the Father can be based.

In the gospels, Jesus continuously identified himself as the Son of man; rather than the Son of God. In fact, some 82 times it is recorded. Certainly this should command special attention. It has been said, if Satan could rid the Bible of the first eleven chapters of the Book of Genesis where man sinned through disobedience to God; and lost his inheritance to Satan, the balance of the Bible would be meaningless. We would not have the covering of Genesis 3:21 or the Messianic promise of Genesis 3:15, wherein God reveals His answer to sin, a virgin-born man who would be our Redeemer.

Jesus, a man, took back our inheritance which Adam lost to Satan. Without Jesus there would be no basis for the grace of the New Testament. Without Jesus the first eleven chapters of the Bible; where we find the foundational doctrines of God's plan for reconciling man unto himself. Without Jesus we would all perish. Without Jesus we would have no example, nor purpose. Without Jesus we would be doomed to an eternity of separation from God. Behold the Man!

Jay R. Leach
Fayetteville, NC
2011

CONTENTS

SECTION 5 – Equipping the Saints

SECTION I

WHY A MAN?

CHAPTER 1

The Beginning: Eden

The beginning phrase of the Bible is *"In the beginning God"*. God is in the beginning. God is the beginning. God was before the beginning. Therefore, God is the source of all that came in the beginning and has ownership and rule of all that comes during and after the beginning. The rest of the story is He, *created the heavens and the earth.* Meaning not only did He create the elements but everything contained there in, on, and there under it; so we see from the Book of Genesis, the beginnings. The theme of not only the Book of Genesis, but the Old Testament is given in Genesis 5:1: This is the book of the generations of Adam. The Old Testament gives the history of Adam and his family.

The Scriptures says, God created man in His own image; and gave him stewardship of the Garden of Eden. But man sinned, thus defiling and defacing that image. Sin in Adam separated him from God, his Creator, and caused the loss of his God-given dominion. Man now Adam and Eve, brought forth children in his likeness and after his image (see Genesis 5:3). Their children proved to have inherited the sin of their parents. Therefore, throughout the Old Testament, we find sin and sinners.

The New Testament on the other hand is the book of the generations of Jesus Christ (see Matthew 1:1). Jesus is the last Adam (see 1 Corinthians

15:45), and He came to earth to save the generations of the first Adam. We should stop and praise God right now; because that saving includes us!

By our natural birth into this world, we were born into the generations of Adam; which means we were born sinners. Oh! But praise God, by His grace we don't have to die one. Through the choice of repentance toward God, faith in Jesus Christ and His finished work, we can be born again, this time into the generations of Jesus Christ and become children of God.

Reading through the genealogy in Genesis 5, is similar to reading the obituary column of a local newspaper, the repeated phrase and he or she died. The Old Testament amplifies the truth, *the wages of sin is death (Romans 6:23)*. But when we turn to the New Testament, the first genealogy emphasizes birth and not death. The theme of the New Testament is, *the gift of God is eternal life through Jesus Christ our Lord (Romans 6:23)*.

The Old Testament is a book of promises while the New Testament is a book of fulfillment. In Genesis 3:15, the so called proto-evangel verse, we find God's first promise of a *Redeemer*, Jesus Christ, is the *fulfillment* of that promise. The word fulfilled in reference to Jesus Christ is very prominent in the Bible. It will come up frequently. Jesus fulfilled the Old Testament promises concerning the *Messiah*. His *birth* was fulfilled in Isaiah 7:14 where we read: *Therefore the Lord Himself will give you a sign: Behold the virgin shall conceive and bear a Son, and shall call His name Immanuel* (see Matthew 1:22-23). Jesus was taken to Egypt for safety, and this fulfilled Hosea 11:1 (see Matthew 2:13-15). Upon the family's return from Egypt and settling in Nazareth, several Old Testament prophecies were fulfilled (see Matthew 2:22-23).

Each of the four gospels has its own perspective on Christ. He is the King in Matthew. He is the Servant in Mark. He is the Son of man in Luke. He is the Son of God in John. Getting the full picture of God's plan for man's redemption requires a composite not only of all four gospels together, but the entire Bible.

Perhaps you are wondering how God, the Creator of all, could allow sin to invade His perfect creation. The Scriptures tell us, that man was created for God's pleasure and glory (Revelation 4:11). However, Adam's sin alienated him from God.

Back to Eden

Sin, the cause of our predicament defined in the Hebrew means, to break away from just authority, trespass, apostasy, and quarrel, transgress, perverse, revolt or rebel. Sin was introduced by the archangel Lucifer. The Scriptures reveal that God has an everlasting kingdom, and in that kingdom there are created spirit beings called angels. Angels fall into two categories, good angels and evil angels. The good angels are concerned with our welfare, the evil angels are out to cause harm to the human race, by disrupting God's plan of redemption for man. There are approximately three hundred references to angels in the Bible which substantiate their existence. The Hebrew word for angel is malek and simply means "an agent" or "messenger." The Greek word for angel is "angelos;" which also means "messenger."

Lucifer

Lucifer means "Light Bearer" or "Son of the Morning" (see Isaiah 14:12-14; Ezekiel 28:11-17; Ephesians 2:2). Lucifer is seen as the archangel who was associated with the throne of God, as leader of the worship of God among the angelic hosts. Through pride and rebellion he fell from that place. Just as various titles and names of God are used to bring out various aspects of

His nature, being, and ministry, so are the designations by which Lucifer now Satan or the devil is known. Two main passages of Scripture describe Satan's origin and fall (Ezekiel 28:1-19; Isaiah 14:4-23).

Daniel's prophecy confirms the fact that there are princes of Satan's kingdom behind the princes of the world kingdoms (see Daniel 8:20-21; 10:10-13; 20-21). Ezekiel 28:1-19; and Isaiah 14:4-23 should be read carefully. It is from these passages mainly that the following description of Satan, prior to his fall is given:

1. Satan is a real personality. He is evil personified and characteristics are ascribed to him. Satan is not an impersonal influence or power. Personal pronouns, intelligence, knowledge, will, and action, are attributed to him (see Job 1:8; 2:1-2; Zechariah 3:1; II Corinthians 2:11; Matthew 4:6; Revelation 12:12; II Timothy 2:26; Matthew 25:41; Isaiah 14:12-13).

2. Satan is a spirit being. Even angels are spirit beings; as God is a Spirit being so is Satan.

3. He is a created being, therefore dependent upon God for his very existence (see Ezekiel 28:13-15).

4. He was an anointed cherub in the heavenly sanctuary, as were the Old Testament prophets, priests, and kings anointed for office (see Ezekiel 28:12, 16, 18).

5. He was the covering Cherub placed by God to cover the throne. Compare this with the Cherubim on the Ark of the Covenant in the tabernacle covering the mercy seat (see Exodus 37:9; Ezekiel 28:14-16).

6. He was in Eden, the garden of God (see Ezekiel 28:15).

7. He was in the holy mountain (or kingdom) of God, in the sides of the north (see Ezekiel 28:14, 16, with Psalm 48:1).

8. He was perfect in the day he was created (see Ezekiel 28:15).

9. He was full of wisdom (see Ezekiel 28:12; with James 3:15-16).

10. He was perfect in beauty (see Ezekiel 28:12).

11. He was decked with precious stones set in gold very similar to the stones in the breastplate of Aaron, Israel's High Priest (see Ezekiel 28:13 with Exodus 28:15-21).

12. He was once in the truth (see John 8:44).

Lucifer's Fall

These same passages, along with other helpful references, show the cause of Satan's fall and those angels that fell with him.

1. He was lifted up in pride over his God-given wisdom, anointing and beauty (see Ezekiel 28:17; Proverbs 16:18; 18:12; 1Timothy 3:6).

2. He exalted himself and came under condemnation (see Isaiah 14:13-14 with 1 Timothy 3:6).

3. He manifested self-will against God's will (see Isaiah 14:13-15).

4. Note the five "I will's" of Lucifer's ambition (see Isaiah 14:13):

   • I will ascend into heaven (self-will).

- I will exalt my throne above the stars of God (self-exaltation).

- I will sit also upon the mount of the congregation in the sides of the north (self enthronement).

- I will ascend above the heights of the clouds (self-ascension).

- I will be like the Most High (self-deification).

5. He fell through pride and self-will, the very essence of sin; and he wanted to be independent of God. He rebelled against God (see Isaiah 14:12 with Proverbs 16:18 and Luke 10:18).

6. He fell as lightening (see Luke 10:18; with II Corinthians 11:14).

7. He was also cast down by God in his self-deification (See Ezekiel 28:16-17).

8. He was the original sinner, and iniquity was found in him (see Ezekiel 28:15, 16, 18; I John 3:8).

9. He did not abide in the truth. He was self-deceived (see John 8:44).

10. He became a liar and a murderer (see John 8:44).

11. He is the source of all sin and in him it is personified. He is the original antichrist. He was the first apostate and he caused other angels to sin in heaven (see II Thessalonians 2:7; Genesis 3:1-6).

12. He was permitted to retain his God-given wisdom which became corrupted and is used by him to deceive mankind today (see Ezekiel 28:17, 18; James 3:15).

13. He will eventually be destroyed in an eternal fire prepared for him and his demons (see Ezekiel 28:18; Matthew 25:41).

Satan's Activity

It becomes evident through examining the Scriptures; that the majority of Satan's activities are centered on deception. It should also be noted that Satan's activities are limited by God especially toward His children. This is seen clearly in the experience of Job as Satan attacked him personally, his household and possessions (see Job 1-2; Luke 22:31; I Corinthians 5:5; I Timothy 1:20).

Though Satan is mighty, he is not All-mighty; though he is wise, he is not All-wise, though he knows, he is not All-knowing, though he is powerful, he is not All-powerful. Nor is he everywhere present. He is subject to his Creator and can only go as far as God permits in affecting mankind.

Biblical Teaching on the Origin of Sin

The Bible points out that man's sin originated in an abuse of the freedom afforded the will of the created. Freedom of the will is the very essence of the rational personality. It includes freedom of activity and also the choice of the end of that activity. Thus, indicating that in the creation, God gave man and for awhile I believe all angels the freedom to voluntarily choose their destiny.

Moral action and freedom to choose requires a law by which character is determined. Otherwise there would be no moral standard. Therefore, neither reward nor punishment could be meted out for either obedience or disobedience. Thus the abuse of free-will and origination of man's sin is found in the Scriptural record of the fall of man. Man was tempted by the serpent (Satan) which indicates that moral evil existed prior to the appearance of the human race and outside of it: *For if God did not spare the angels who sinned, but cast them down to hell and delivered them into chains of darkness, to be reserved for judgment (2 Peter 2:4).*

The account of the probation and fall of man is an accurate record of fact (see Genesis 3:1-24). The biblical account reveals that, while man was created in innocence and holiness, there existed the possibility of sin. Otherwise men and angels would have been like mere robots. The immediate consequences of man's sin were separation from God and enslavement to Satan, together with the loss of his dominion. With these losses man became subject to physical and moral corruption.

God planted many trees in the Garden of Eden but in the midst of the garden that is in a special place, He planted two trees, the tree of life and the tree of the knowledge of good and evil. Adam created in innocence; had no knowledge of good and evil (see Genesis 2:8-9).

"Now the garden is full of trees, which are full of fruits, you may eat of the fruit of every tree freely except the tree of the knowledge of good and evil. You must not eat of that tree, for in the day that you do you will surely die" (see Genesis 2:15-17). Adjacent to the tree of the knowledge of good and evil stands the tree of life. Earlier, we said Adam was created innocent, that is, between the tree of life (life) and the tree of the knowledge of good and evil (death). God put these two trees there so that Adam might exercise free-will, choice. He could choose either.

The tree of the knowledge of good and evil, though forbidden to Adam is not wrong in itself. In a sense Adam was limited as he could not decide for himself on moral issues. Judgment of right and wrong didn't reside in him, but in God; so when faced with any question he had to refer it to God. Thus, his life was totally dependent on God. Here we are presented a picture of God's eternal plan for the life of man, the divine and the human.

If Adam should choose the tree of life, he would partake of the life of God. Thus he would become a son of God, as his life is derived from God. The results would be the union of God's life with man, a new creation, having the life of God in them and living in total dependence upon God for that life. I will expound on this point in a later chapter.

However, Adam turned the other way, to the tree of the knowledge of good and evil (see Genesis 3:6). In so doing he became independent and without the life of God. Now, he could command knowledge and he could decide the issues for himself. He was wise. Yet, true to God's Word the consequence of that choice for him was death rather than life. This choice also put him in league with Satan's plan to shatter God's eternal plan for man, and therefore fell under the judgment of God. Because of his choice, we all became sinners, equally dominated by Satan, and equally deserving the wrath of God. The history of humanity is the outcome of Adam's choice.

Because of His love for Adam and Eve, God expelled them from the Garden of Eden rather than allow them to remain and eventually eat of the tree of life; which would have alienated, and separated them in their sinful state eternally. Adam was created in the image of God. That image was defaced but not totally lost as was the case with initial holiness and innocence into which they had been created. Notice God continues to interact with them in their sinful state, that's love! That love for man has not abated. While He does not love sin; He continues to love sinners. What a mighty God we serve! (see Genesis 1:26-27; 5:3; 9:6).

Depravity

Deprived of the relationship with God for which he and his descendents have been created; the condition of Adam and his descendents became one of depravity. That is original sin, the corruption of the nature of all of the off springs of Adam. Therefore every one is very far gone from original righteousness. The effect of the fall on the human race is described in the Scriptures as the universal reality of death, together with a positive bias of human nature towards evil.

It has been said that man uses little more than 10% of his brain capacity. Certainly immediately upon leaving the Garden man's use of his brain capacity was significantly higher perhaps 90% or more. When we consider the numerous unexplained accomplishments of prior civilizations like the tower of Babel (see Genesis 6), and the pyramids of Egypt, we know that a higher capacity was necessary. However, as man became weaker and wiser naturally with the passing of time he progressively lost and continues to lose his godly wisdom and strength.

Many of the attempts to provide an explanation for the origin of sin are humanistic and rationalistic however, the last Word on sin is spoken by God, in His plan of redemptive grace as the remedy, a man for man's sin.

Personal Journal Notes
(Reflection & Responses)

1. The most important thing I learned from this chapter was:

2. The area that I need to work on the most is:

3. I can apply this lesson to my life by:

4. Closing statement of Commitment

CHAPTER 2

Representative Heads: God's Plan for Man's Sin

*T*herefore, *just as through one man sin entered the world, and death through sin, and thus death spread to all men, because all sinned. For until the law sin was in the world, but sin is not imputed when there is no law. Nevertheless, death reigned from Adam to Moses, even those who had not sinned according to the likeness of the transgression of Adam, who was a type of Him who was to come. But the free gift is not like the offense. For if by the one man's offense many died, much more the grace of God and the gift by the grace of the one Man, Jesus Christ, abounded to many. And the gift is not like that which came through the one that sinned. For the judgment which came from one offense resulted in condemnation, but the free gift which came from many offenses resulted in justification. For if by one man's offense death reined through the one, much more those who receive abundance of grace and of the gift of righteousness will rein in life through the One, Jesus Christ. Therefore, as through one man's offense judgment came to all men, resulting in condemnation, even so through one Man's righteous act the free gift came to all men, resulting in justification of life (Romans 5:12-18).* Behold the Man!

Verse 18 summarizes Paul's teaching above. One act of one man brought sin and its penalty of death upon the human race. On the other hand, the obedience of one man counteracted that deed and made righteousness and eternal life available to mankind.

Adam headed the old humanity characterized by sin and death. Jesus Christ heads a new humanity characterized by righteousness and life. We come under the consequences of Adam's sin by natural descent. We come under Christ's obedience by regeneration and faith (see John 3:3; 1 Corinthians 15:22; 2 Corinthians 5:14).

Paul refers to Adam as a type of Christ and draws an analogy between Adam and Christ (v. 14). They are similar in the fact that their deeds affected many people. However, their differences are more pronounced and Paul gives a threefold contrast:

- Adam's act was an offense, a deliberate going away; while Christ's deed was one of grace.

- Adam's sin resulted in condemnation and death; whereas, Christ's deed of grace brought justification and life (vv. 16, 17).

- Adam is characterized by disobedience, while Christ is characterized by obedience (vv. 18, 19).

The passage of Scripture, Romans 5:12-18, along with vv. 19-21, must be understood within the context Romans 3:21-5:11, which sets forth the gospel of the grace, the undeserved favor of God as revealed through Jesus Christ.

A summary of God's plan of representative heads for the human race: Adam sinned once and all whom Adam represented were found guilty. Christ obeyed throughout His whole life and all whom Christ represented will be made righteous.

Some object to this idea of representative heads for the human race. But if we do not think it fair that we were counted guilty for Adam's disobedience, then we also should not think it fair that we are counted righteous for Christ's obedience.

God So Loved

Genesis 3:1-24, the chapter covering the fall of man introduces two dominant themes of Old Testament theology:

- God is redemptive and personal.

And I will put enmity between you and the woman, and between your seed and her seed; He shall bruise your head, and you shall bruise His heel (v. 15). New Testament allusions to v. 15 indicate that the curse to the serpent has a broader application. Interpreted messianically, enmity represents the conflict between Satan (your seed) and God's people, especially Jesus Christ (her Seed). He shall bruise your head, and you shall bruise His heel depicts the long struggle between good and evil, with God ultimately winning through Jesus Christ, the last Adam (see Romans 16:20; Hebrews 2:14; Revelation 12).

V.15 is often referred to as the first messianic prophecy in the Old Testament, the proto-evangel. Through disobedience to the terms of his rule man falls, thus experiencing the loss of his dominion (vv. 22, 23). Everything of his delegated realm comes under a curse as his relationship with God, the Source, of his rule is severed (vv. 17, 18). Therefore, man loses the life power, essential to ruling in God's kingdom (vv. 19, 22).

Through his disobedience and submission to the serpent, man forfeited his rule to the serpent. The Bible verifies that the spirit taking the snake's form is Satan himself (See Revelation 12:9). A second fact offers hope amid the tragedy. God begins to move in redemption, and a plan for recovering man's lost estate is promised and set in motion with the first sacrifice requiring the shedding of blood; which remains the dominate factor in redemption throughout man's earthly experience (vv. 15, 21).

- Man is sinful.

And for Adam and his wife the Lord made tunics of skin, and clothed them (Genesis 3:21). The Covenant love of God required the blood sacrifice of innocent animals to provide skin as a covering for Adam and Eve. This early foreshadowing of substitutionary atonement points to the necessary judgment upon the innocent to provide a covering for the guilty.

Adam and Eve made an attempt to cover themselves by sewing together fig leaves. However, God's order provided covering by means of a sacrifice, not without blood. Under the new covenant, we are required to be clothed with Christ (see Galatians 3:27; Hebrews 9:12; Matthew 26:28).

The curse is reinforced by Adam and Eve being expelled from the Garden, where they had walked in the cool of the evening in full communion with the Lord God. Cherubim, with a flaming sword which turned every way, prevented their return, but I repeat this prevention was because of God's love for them, not His wrath (Genesis 3:22, 24).

Personal Journal Notes
(Reflection & Responses)

1. The most important thing that I learned from this chapter was:

2. The area that I need to work on the most is:

3. I can apply this lesson to my life by:

4. Closing Statement of Commitment:

CHAPTER 3

Justification: God's Redemptive Purpose

The principal concern of the Bible is the redemption of man and his reconciliation back to God. For that reason God raised up a nation, Israel, a people to whom He could speak by His prophets and through whom He could prepare a Savior.

Therefore, as through one man's offense judgment came to all men, resulting in condemnation, even so through one Man's righteous act the free gift came to all men, resulting in justification of life (Romans 5:19).

What Jesus accomplished for us in His life, death, and resurrection, the Holy Spirit seeks to make a reality in us. Despite very real and substantial differences among Christians, those in truth agree that man is in need of salvation not from his weaknesses, but from a moral problem, sin. They also agree that this salvation is by grace through faith in the finished work of our Lord and Savior, Jesus Christ, rather than through man's self-improvement. Salvation results from certain radical changes in man's nature as he partakes of the divine nature of God. These changes are seen in his actual moral character and spiritual condition. Before the new birth it is man's nature to run to sin; however, after the new birth it becomes his nature to run away from sin.

For I delivered to you first of all that which I received: that Christ died for our sins according to the Scriptures, and that He was buried, and that He rose again the third day according to the Scriptures (1 Corinthians 15:3-4). The concern of this chapter will be to describe the first steps in the process whereby a sinner, rebellious, and without spiritual life, becomes a child of God, reconciled, forgiven, and a new creature in Christ Jesus (see Ephesians 4:24; 2 Corinthians 5:12-21; Ephesians 1:13).

The First Step

The Scriptures reveal that God takes the first step in the redemption of men. A few months ago the news media began reporting the saga of a group of men in Chile trapped in a mine about a half mile or so down in the earth. Though told that it may take months to rescue them, they waited because they knew their only hope was from the outside. Thank God all of them were rescued. Man, as these men, is entombed under the bondage of sin, and his only hope of rescue is outside. God, by His grace, is seeking to rescue man. The first step is God's. If a man is ever saved, it must be through the grace and power of God; which God extended to all men through Jesus Christ (see John 3:16; Matthew 6:33).

Salvation through Grace

Grace has been defined as unmerited favor of God. It has also been described as God's personal attitude toward man, through His action and influence upon him. This grace of God is the fountain of all our blessings, but particularly to the salvation of man. *For by grace you have been saved through faith, and that not of yourselves; it is the gift of God (Ephesians 2:8, 10-22).*

The Holy Spirit is God dynamically present with man. The Scriptures say, God has poured His Spirit out on all flesh; this fact should dispel the belief of so many people, who interpret this passage to refer only to those in the leadership of the church (see Joel 2:28; Acts 2:17). However, we know that the Holy Spirit communicates the grace of God to us. It is by the Spirit that God calls us to salvation, convicts us of sin and awakens us to our need. It is by the power of the Holy Spirit that people turn unto Christ in repentance and faith, and it is by the Spirit that people are born again and renewed in the image of God. *And you He made alive, who were dead in trespasses and sin (Ephesians 2:1).*

If a person is indeed dead in trespasses and sins he or she cannot turn and prepare themselves through their own natural strength and works to faith and calling unto God, how can they be saved? In John 3:16 we read, *For God so loved the world that He gave His only begotten Son, that whoever believes in Him should not perish but have everlasting life.*

The first step in reconciliation is a universal bestowment of the grace of God to all men. *But God demonstrates His own love toward us, in that while we were still sinners, Christ died for us (Romans 5:8).* Thus, enabling all men who will turn from sin to righteousness, believe on Jesus Christ for forgiveness and cleansing from sin; and follow good works pleasing and acceptable in His sight (see Romans10:9-10; John 17:17, also John 15:1-8).

Pray, *Lord Jesus Christ, Son of God made man, have mercy on me, a sinner. Forgive me for all unrighteousness, and cleanse me by your precious Blood. Amen.*

What is Man to Believe?
Daily we see more and more rejection of Christianity across this Nation. Everywhere there is an increase of new beliefs and religions being recognized. What was on Adam and Eve's minds when they realized that they were naked before a Holy God? Certainly it was not to ask Him for advice as indicated by what they did next. They tried to cover their nakedness with

fig leaves. Having eaten from the tree of the knowledge of good and evil, Adam now has a conscience which tells him right from wrong and his guilt naturally drives him to seek his own solution independent of God.

Think of the predicament Adam and Eve would have found themselves in eternally had God Himself not rescued them. How? He rescued them through the shedding of blood; when He killed animals and made tunics of skin to cover them; then in love, He drove them from the Garden, lest they partake of the tree of life, and live eternally in their sinful state (see Genesis 3:21-22). God continues to this day to hate sin, but He also continues to love the sinner.

This early foreshadowing of *substitution atonement* points toward the necessity of judgment upon the innocent to provide a covering for the guilty. Adam and Eve made a vain attempt to cover themselves through their own efforts. So it is today with the many fig leaf religions spreading themselves across this great land. However, God's order provided a covering by means of a *sacrifice*. Under the new covenant, we are required to be *clothed* with Christ rather than with our good works (see Galatians 3:27). So God established His way of restoring man in the very beginning, not without blood (see Hebrews 9:7). It will become clear that there is no single Scriptural idea, stretching from Genesis to Revelation, more constantly and more prominently kept in view than that expressed by the words, the blood.

Beyond Eden

The Scriptural record about the blood begins just outside the gate of Eden. It begins with the sacrifice of Abel. He brought *the firstlings of his flock* (see Genesis 4:4) to the Lord as a sacrifice, and there in connection with the first act of worship recorded in the Bible, blood was shed. The question is answered here concerning the rejection by God of Cain's offering. *In the process of time it came to pass that Cain brought an offering of the fruit of the ground to the Lord. Abel also brought of the firstborn of his flock and of their fat. And the Lord respected Abel and his offering (Genesis 4:3-4).*

Notice, the word *"also"* indicates that Abel brought the same offering as Cain; but he also brought the firstborn of his flock. Cain's vegetables alone like his father's fig leaves were his own bloodless efforts. I'm sure that Adam taught both of them what was required in bringing offerings to God. Additionally, they both probably observed their father's offerings, which he no doubt learned from God Himself (see Genesis 3:21). We get further understanding of their offerings in Hebrews 11, where we read of Abel's offerings, *God testifying of his gifts; and through it he being dead still speaks (v. 4).* The writer of Hebrews records Abel's offerings as gifts not as a single gift. In Genesis 4:3, Cain brought a single offering of fruit, a gift.

Again, in Hebrews 11:4, we learn that it was *by faith* that Abel offered an acceptable sacrifice, and his name stands first in the record of those whom the Bible calls believers. He had this witness given to him *that he was righteous.* His faith and God's pleasure with it are closely connected with the sacrificial blood. This testimony given at the very beginning of human history is of deep significance.

We see from this revelation that there can be no approach to God, no fellowship with Him by faith, or enjoyment of His favor without the shedding of blood. The first recorded act of Noah, upon leaving the ark was the offering of a burnt sacrifice to God. As it was with Abel, so it was with Noah, not without shedding of blood.

Then we have the divine call of Abraham and the miraculous birth of Isaac. God was forming a people to serve Him. But again, the purpose could not be accomplished without the shedding of blood. God had already entered into a covenant relationship with Abraham, his faith had been tried and he stood the test. The Scripture says, *"It was reckoned, or counted to him for righteousness"* (see Romans 4:9).

Yet he had to learn that Isaac, his son of promise, who belonged wholly to God, could be surrendered to God only through death. Isaac had to die! Upon a mount in the land of Moriah, Abraham had to offer Isaac on the altar at God's command (see Genesis 22:1-18). It was the revelation of a divine truth, *that only through death is it possible for a life to be truly consecrated to God.* But because of sin, it was impossible for Isaac to die and rise again from the dead. The Scriptures tell us that *Isaac's life was spared and a ram was offered in his stead (see verse 13).* Through the blood of the ram in the bush that flowed on Mount Moriah, Isaac's life was spared. By that blood in a sense he was raised from the dead. We see the great lesson of *substitution* taught here by Almighty God who also provided the ram. Satan has since the inception of substitution worked passionately to divert man to a religion of works and goodness. He and his demons are working overtime to blind the church of the necessity of this principle of substitution, *not without blood* (see Hebrews 9:7).

Four hundred years later, we see Isaac in Egypt. He is now the people of Israel. Through God's mighty deliverance from Egyptian bondage, Israel is to become recognized as God's firstborn among the nations. Here again, this deliverance was *not without blood.*

What God had accomplished through the blood on Mount Moriah for one person, Abraham, who was the father of the nation, now has to be experienced by that nation. This was accomplished through the sprinkling of the door frames of the Israelites' homes with the *shed blood of a lamb* and by the *institution of the Passover, wherein they ate the flesh of the slain lamb, as a perpetual ordinance* with the words, *"When I see the blood I will pass over you" (Exodus 12:13).* The children of Israel were taught that day that life can be obtained only by the death of a substitute. Life was possible, but only through the blood given in their place, and this life could be taken hold of by the sprinkling of that blood.

Israel reached Mount Sinai. God called Moses up into the Mount were He gave him His law, the Ten Commandments (See Exodus 20) as the foundation of His covenant. Notice this time the blood is not placed on the altar, nor the doorposts, but on the people themselves and the Book (See Exodus 24:8). God wants us to know, *"It is the blood that makes atonement for the soul" (Leviticus 17:11).*

Immediately after the establishment of the covenant, God gave the command, *"Let them make Me a sanctuary, that I may dwell among them" (Exodus 25:8).* They were to enjoy the full blessing of having the God of the covenant abiding among them. Listen, through His grace, they could find Him and serve Him in His house.

God Himself gave Moses the instructions for the tabernacle at the same time He gave Him the Ten Commandments in the mount. These instructions were to be carried out to the minutest detail, concerning the construction, arrangement, and the service of that house. He left nothing to the mind of man. But you will notice that the blood is the center focus and reason for all. See **Figure #1** below:

Figure #1

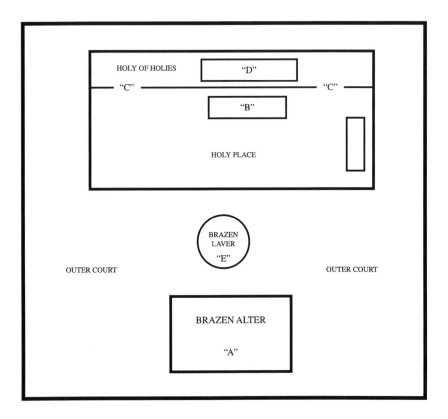

At the very entrance to this House of God, and the first thing visible in the outer court was the *brazen altar.* **("A" in Figure #1).** Here the sprinkling of blood continued, without ceasing, from morning until evening. Outside the gate the bearer brought his sacrifice, laid his hands on its head to identify with it; then slew it and presented it to the priest as a substitute for his sins and those of his family. The priest in turn flayed the sacrifice and placed it upon the brazen altar to be consumed by fire. The blood was sprinkled on each of the horns; one located on each of the four corners of the altar (See Genesis 12:7) symbolizing power, the remainder of the blood was poured out at the base of the altar. Enter the Holy Place and the most conspicuous thing is the *golden altar of incense* **("B" in Figure**

#1) which also, together with the *veil* (**"C" in Figure #1**) was constantly sprinkled with the blood. And situated beyond the Holy Place is the Holy of Holies where God dwelled. The *mercy seat* (**"D" in Figure #1**) *of the ark of the covenant* where His glory shined was also sprinkled with the blood once every year when the high priest alone entered the Holy of Holies, and into God's presence, which is the picture of heaven itself, *but not without blood* (See Hebrews 9:7).

Please take note, the one absolute essential that we must have to be able to stand before God is not our church membership, baptism, confirmation, or good works. *It is the blood of Christ.* We must come to God, not without blood, *"for without shedding of blood is no remission"* (see Hebrews 9:22). The highest act in that worship was the sprinkling of the blood. All of those Old Testament sacrifices were pointing toward the sacrifice that Jesus was going to make (see Hebrews 9:13-14). Be sure that you apply Christ's blood by faith to your heart and life so that God sees it as the atonement for your sins.

In the Old Testament a lamb was offered to God in payment for sin continued for fifteen hundred years. At Mt. Sinai, in the desert, at Shiloh, in the temple on Mount Moriah, it continued. The picture made by our Lord on Calvary brings to an end all of the shadows by His bringing in the substance and establishing a fellowship with the Holy One in spirit and in truth. Behold the Man! Christ suffered and died for our sins, and now you can stand boldly before God, completely washed from all sin, if you claim Christ and His sacrifice for yourself.

Behold the Man

When Jesus Christ came, *"Old things passed away and all things, became new" (see 2 Corinthians 5:17).* He came from the Father in heaven and He is the way, the only way to the Father and the heaven from whence He came. The Lord Jesus Christ Himself plainly declared that His death on the cross was the purpose for which He came into the world; and that it was a *necessary* condition for redemption and the eternal life that He brought. John the Baptist made an accurate assessment, *"Behold the Lamb of God, who takes away the sin of the world!" (see John 1:29)*. He was born in a stable; what an appropriate place for a lamb to be born. So there was no room in the inn for such a birth. Jesus clearly stated that, in connection with His death, the shedding of His blood was necessary.

After the Resurrection
After His resurrection and ascension, our Lord was no longer known by the apostles *"after the flesh" (2 Corinthians 5:16)*. All that was symbolic had passed away, and the deep spiritual truths expressed symbolically were unveiled. But there is no passing of the blood it continues to occupy its place of prominence. After our new birth, we are no longer to be known after the flesh for we now walk as we are led by the Spirit (See Romans 8:1; John 14: 12-21).

The epistle to the Hebrews was written intentionally to show them that the temple sacrifice had become obsolete and was intended by God to pass away, now that Christ had come. Here it might be expected that the Holy Spirit would emphasize the true spirituality of God's purpose, yet it is just here that the blood of Jesus is spoken of in a manner that imparts a new value to the phrase.

We read that *"with His own blood He entered the holy place once for all"* (Hebrews 9:12). That's good news! You and I don't deserve it, but God isn't giving us what we do deserve. God is not angry with us nor is He holding our sins against us. Jesus entered into the Holy Place *"once for all"* and obtained for us eternal redemption. Listen, He paid for *all of your sins past, present, and even those you have not committed yet*. Our part is to accept what He has done by faith.

As stated in an earlier chapter, we should stop identifying ourselves as sinners. For one to say that he or she is sinner saved by grace leaves so much lacking in this life giving experience; as believers, we are no longer in that camp. He or she is a new creature, old things are passed away, behold all things are become new (See 2 Corinthians 5:17) with a new nature (See 2 Peter 1:4). We will not live like the devil. Now he or she loves the Lord Jesus and certainly won't want to mistreat Him any more than they would want to mistreat their loved one.

The other side of that is the person who says, he or she is saved and then still lives like the devil himself is simply proving that he or she is still the devil's child (See 1 John 2:19). Therefore, the believer does not come under the same judgment the unbelievers do. We are to judge ourselves or know that God will judge us and chastise us if we fail to judge ourselves (See 1 Corinthians 11:31-32). Instead of walking on egg shells thinking you are going to hell, by faith turn to the Savior and His Word and get it right (See Romans 10:9-10; 1 John 1:9; 2:1-2).

Concerning our Lord, we read that *"the blood of Christ, cleanse your conscience* (verse 14). *Therefore brethren, having boldness to enter the holiest by the blood of Jesus* Hebrews 10:19). *You have come to Jesus the Mediator of the New Covenant, and to the blood of sprinkling* (Hebrews 12:22, 24). *Jesus also, that He might sanctify the people with His own blood, suffered outside the gate* (Hebrews 13:12). *"God brought up from the dead our Lord Jesus, that great Shepherd of the sheep, through the blood of the everlasting Covenant"* (verse 20). By such words, the Holy Spirit teaches us that the blood is really the central power of our entire redemption; not without blood is as valid in the New Testament as in the Old Testament. Nothing but the blood of Jesus shed in His death for sin can cover sin on God's side or wash it away on ours.

We find the same teaching in the writings of the apostles. Paul wrote of *being justified freely by His grace through the redemption that is in Christ Jesus … through faith in His blood* (Romans 3:24-26), and of *being now justified by His blood* (Romans 5:9).

Peter reminded his readers that they were the *"elect unto obedience and sprinkling of the blood of Jesus Christ"* (1 Peter 1:2), that they were redeemed by *"the precious blood of Jesus Christ"* (verse 19).

John assured his *little children* (1 John 2:1) that *the blood of Jesus Christ His Son cleanses us from all sin* (1 John 1:7). The Son is He *who came … not only by water, but by water and blood* (1 John 5:6).

I Know it was the Blood

When John the Baptist announced Jesus' coming, he spoke of Him as filling a dual office: as *"the Lamb of God, who takes away the sin of the world"* (see John 1:29) and then as *"He which baptizeth with the Holy Ghost and with fire" KJV* (John 1:33). The outpouring of the blood of the Lamb of God had to take place before the outpouring of the Holy Spirit could be bestowed. Only after all that the Old Testament taught about the *blood* had been fulfilled could the dispensation of the Holy Spirit begin.

In the synagogue at Capernaum, Jesus spoke of Himself as the *"bread of life* (See John 6:35, 48); of His flesh, He said that He would *"give [it] for the life of the world"* (verse 51). He said most emphatically: *"Unless you eat the flesh of the Son of Man and drink His blood, you have no life in you." "Whoever eats My flesh and drinks My blood has eternal life, and I will raise him up in the last day. He who eats My flesh and drinks My blood abides in Me, and I in him"* (see verses 53-56). Our Lord thus declared the foundational fact that He Himself, the Son of Man, the Son of the Father, who came into the world born of a virgin, to restore to us our lost life could do this in no other way than by dying for us, by shedding His blood for us [man for man], and then by making us partakers of its power (see 2 Corinthians 5:21). Equally noticeable is our Lord's declaration of the same truth on the last night of His earthly life. Before He completed the great work of His life by giving it as a ransom for many (see Matthew 20:28).

Holy Communion

Jesus instituted the Lord's Supper, saying, *"Drink ye all of it; for this is My blood of the new testament, which is shed for many for the remission of sins* (Matthew 26:27-28) KJV. Jesus did not set a scheduled date or time, we are to commune, but when we do we are to remember Him in all of His work. I've noticed in my own travels across this nation and abroad, some churches commune daily, while others commune weekly, monthly or even quarterly. However, to many it is just a ceremony, a tradition, or an act. God forbid!

From communion, we get the words community and unity all of which points to oneness. This was Jesus' prayer in John 17, that we would be one. This should be the focus of every local church, once attained we are prepared for His service and much can be accomplished in the natural realm and spiritual realm. However, our oneness or unity in the Communion service should manifest God's power through healing. Not only should we review the familiar scriptural passages used with communion services (see Matthew 26:26-28; Mark 14:22-35; Luke 22:19, 20, and 1 Corinthian 11:23-26); but we should incorporate these passages from Isaiah: *As many were astonished at thee; His visage was so marred more than any man, and his form more than the sons of men (Isaiah 52:14). And with His stripes we are healed (Isaiah 53:5) KJV.*

In our remembrance of Jesus on the cross, Isaiah reported that His appearance was marred, and grotesque indicating that He was unrecognizable even as a human. It was not the beating with many stripes and nails only, but I believe He also carried our sickness and diseases like cancers, arthritis, and all others sicknesses and diseases were laid on Him. Therefore, *with his stripes we are healed.*

"Without shedding of blood there is no remission" (see Hebrews 9:22). By the shedding of His blood, Jesus has obtained a new life for us. By what He calls "the drinking of His blood," He shares His life with us. The blood shed in the atonement frees us from the guilt of sin, from death, punishment of sin, and the curse; which includes the fore-mentioned diseases. The blood of the Man, Jesus Christ, which we drink by faith, bestows His life on us. It seems so easy for us to believe that our sins were forgiven through Christ's blood shed at Calvary. But why is it so hard for us to believe that the power of His blood shed to redeem us, also delivered us from the curse? (see Galatians 3:10-14, 18; also Romans 14:13, 14).

As a Man thinks in his Heart

Proverbs 23:7 says, "For as he thinks in his heart so is he." The Scriptures also states that the truth shall set you free. That is, the truth you know, that sets you free. I believe in divine healing and the keeping power of the Holy Spirit. It's in my heart and I live it every day trusting God to keep me healthy along with all other provisions needed to fulfill my assignment. In June 2010, I stepped down from the pulpit after 28 continuous years in the pastorate, never missing a Sunday because of sickness or disease. Immediately, my wife and I moved to full-time ministry in the Bread of Life Ministries, an equipping ministry we founded in 1998. Our mission through planting churches and establishing non-traditional Bible Institute campuses is: *"teaching them to observe all things that I have commanded you"* (see Matthew 28:20). We take our example from the apostle Paul in

2 Timothy 2:2, *"And these things that you have heard from me among many witnesses, commit these to faithful men who will be able to teach others also."* Here, Paul establishes a pattern for the preservation and transmission of the gospel truths. Apostolic teaching, fellowship, communion, and prayer, are to be passed on to succeeding generations without addition or alteration (see Acts 2:42). While other activities have been added over the centuries; these four elements must be present to have a vital church.

At the Bread of Life Ministries, we view ministry as service and as ministers of the gospel, we are primarily servants of God's Word. We treasure the Word of God; and boldly share its message tirelessly, being careful to communicate its truth with accuracy. This is no easy task, because of the Word of God; we are opposed by many in traditional church circles. For over forty years, my wife and I have carried on a teaching ministry wherever we were located (26 ½ of those years in the military). We opened our home for a weekly teaching ministry at each duty station and soon the group would grow to a point; we would plant a church. However, in many cases a humble pastor would encourage us to establish a Bible teaching ministry within their existing church. Only heaven knows how many churches and ministries around the world and across America have come out our ministry over the years. It is truly a blessing to us as we from time to time get calls, cards, letters and reports from some of those whom God has allowed us to disciple. Thank God for those faithful men and women; who keep our ministry's motto to, "Come Learn and Go Teach"!

I pray that all who are reading this book no matter where you live; already know Jesus as your personal Savior but if not, that you will receive this invitation and accept Him today. There is no better or more opportune time than right now to repent and accept Him. My prayer to God is that you will do that. The Scripture records, *"That if you confess with your mouth the Lord Jesus and believe in your heart that God has raised Him from the dead, you will be saved, for with the heart one believes unto righteousness, and with the mouth confession is made unto salvation" (Romans 10:9, 10).*

Confessing the Lord Jesus is not a simple acknowledgment that He is God and the Lord of the universe, since even demons acknowledge that to be true (see James 2:19). This is a deep personal conviction that you know without reservation that Jesus is your Lord and Savior. This phase also includes your repenting by changing your mind about sin and agreeing with God and His Word about it, trusting Jesus for salvation, and submitting to Him as your Lord and Savior. This is strictly voluntary by faith on your part. Please do it now. We usually think of tomorrow, but tomorrow is not promised to us. Today is the day of salvation.

Continual Confession or Cleansing of Sin

While the false pretender will not admit his or her sin, the genuine Christian admits and forsakes it (see 1 John 1:9). Again, to confess means to say the same thing about sin that God says about it. Continual confession or cleansing of sin indicates a true or genuine salvation experience. The Christian life is referred to repeatedly as a walk. Believers are told in Ephesians to: *Walk worthy of the calling with which you were called (4:1); walk as children of light (5:8); walk in love (5:2); and walk circumspectly (5:15),* just to name a few of the admonitions about the Christian walk. We are to *walk in the light (1:7).* Outside of the light range is darkness. Picture if you will the range of the headlights on your car. You can only see the distance covered by their beams. God's Word is our light, by which we see and walk. I'm sure that we would not attempt to drive in the dark, yet so many walk in darkness because they refuse the light that God has given us through His Spirit and His Word (see Psalm 119:105; John 14:26). The Christian life is also spoken of several times as the way, in the Book of Acts.

In our study of the tabernacle on page 21, we did not cover one item (see the brazen laver **"E" in Figure #1).** In the short distance from the brazen altar to the holy place, the priests would get their sandaled feet dirty and would need to wash them before entering into the holy place to minister. In our walk we sin (miss the mark) and get our hands and feet dirty (walking in the world exposed to defilement) and need them cleansed, so we need the laver, which pictures Christ cleansing us from all worldly defilement (See 1 John 1:9).

A great explanation of this principle is demonstrated in John 13, about foot-washing. When the Lord came to Peter to wash his feet, Peter said, "You will never wash my feet! Jesus answered him, *"If I do not wash you, you have no part in Me" (v.8).* The word for "part" denotes the idea of "fellowship" or "partnership" in activity not "relationship." Peter wanted fellowship; he already had a relationship with Jesus. Therefore he said, "Lord, not my feet only, but also my hands and my head!" (v.9). Jesus answered, *"He who is bathed ["bathed," as the Greek word "louo" means] needs only to wash [Greek, nipto] his feet, but is completely clean" (v.10).* The first word is louo, which means "to bathe all over." The second is nipto, which means "to wash just a part of the body," such as the hands and feet. These words accurately fit the functions of the brazen altar and brazen laver.

He that has been bathed from his sins at the brazen altar, where we see the Cross and Christ judged for our sins in salvation does not need to be bathed again, but simply needs to wash his feet at the brazen laver, where we judge ourselves daily for sins through the Word of God and the Holy Spirit, from the defilement of sins. Then we enter the holy place of worship and service. Jesus was showing Peter that He was going to forgive him for the denial even before he committed the act, as foretold in verse 38.

Hebrews 12:4-11 helps us to understand the Lord's chastening: *For whom the Lord loves He chastens, and scourges every son whom He receives (v.6).* God loves His children, so He chastens them because He does not want them ruined by sin. God does not merely give advice. His Word says, *"He that spares his rod hates his son" (Proverbs 13:24).* God chastens every son whom He receives, for still *"there is none righteous, no not one" (See Romans 3:10).*

If one who professes to be a believer goes on in sin and is not chastened of the Lord, it is because he or she is not really saved at all, not a child of God, according to Hebrews 12:8. God's chastening *is "always for our good, and yields the peaceable fruit of righteousness unto them which is exercised thereby" (v. 11).* The way to escape the chastening of the Lord is to judge ourselves. We simply must examine our lives, and motives daily. When the Holy Spirit shows us sin, we must deal with it. First John 2 says we can judge ourselves when we *"walk in the light (See 1 John 1:7).* We do this by feeding daily on God's Word and allowing the Holy Spirit to throw light on our actions and attitudes. *"If we say that we have no sin, we deceive ourselves, and the truth is not in us" (v.8),* but when we become conscious of our sins and *"we confess our sins, He is faithful and just to forgive us our sins, and cleanse us from all unrighteousness" (v.9).*

We are not to come as some do, saying, *"We have not sinned and thereby make Him a liar" (v.10),* but we are to name the sin to God and trust Him to forgive it that moment. We must keep good records and confess in order to get the joy we once knew.

The people who were told to wash were the priests coming into the tabernacle to minister before the Lord (See Exodus 30:18-21). Only the priests were allowed inside the holy place to worship before the Lord. The priests were born of the tribe of Levi and ordained by the Lord for the tabernacle service. God's Word declares that all who are born of God are His priests today. *But you are a chosen generation, a royal priesthood, a holy nation. His own special people; that you may proclaim the praises of Him who called you out of darkness into His marvelous light (1 Peter 2:9).* We are also called "kings and priests" (See Revelation 1:6). What a glorious truth that each of us has the right to come before God. We are invited by God to come spiritually into the holy place for worship. Not just the select few can pray or worship before Him, but all who are born again into this royal priesthood have the equal privilege to come boldly unto the throne of grace (see Hebrews 4:16).

The ultimate purpose of the brazen laver was for the priests to cleanse themselves so they could go into the holy place. Inside the holy place was the food for the priests, the showbread, the altar of incense, a place of prayer, and the candlestick. These represent spiritual exercises, the Word, prayer and worship, for the believer. The reason most people do not enjoy praying or worshipping the Lord is that they are on the outside, out of fellowship with Him. It is such a serious thing that God warned them twice that they should wash, *"that they die not" (see Exodus 30:20).*

Personal Journal Notes
(Reflection & Response)

1. The most important thing that I learned from this chapter is:

2. The area that I need to work on the most is:

3. I can apply this lesson to my life by:

4. Closing Statement of Commitment

CHAPTER 4

A Summons: The Gospel Call

Hear Jesus' gospel call, *"Come unto Me, all you who labor and are heavy laden, and I will give you rest. Take My yoke upon you and learn of Me, for I am meek and lowly in heart, and you will find rest for your souls. For My yoke is easy and My burden is light"* (Matthew 11:28-30). *"I am the bread of life. He who comes to Me shall never hunger, and he who believes in Me shall never thirst. But I said to you that you have seen Me and yet you do not believe. All that the Father gives Me will come to Me, and the one who comes to Me I will by no means cast out"* (see John 6:35-37, 45; 10:28-29).

The gospel call is just what the words imply: a summons to an individual to accept the gospel. Salvation comes when the individual hears, receives, and heeds the gospel call.

The first step toward salvation is the experience of the Holy Spirit quickening or bringing back to life the human spirit; which was dead due to sin. As stated, this happens when we believe on the Lord Jesus Christ as our Savior. Many times upon this confession we baptize the individual and then accept them into membership of the church. From there the concern seems to turn to a place of working in the church, in many cases with little or no biblical or doctrinal training; but lots of denominational discipline. To be obedient to our Lord's command, the church has the responsibility of equipping this person through teaching and building him or her up in the most holy faith, making them a disciple of Christ, capable of reproducing themselves in others (see Matthew 28:18-20; 2 Timothy 2:2).

Disciple making begins with a renewed mind. We were born into this world before we were reborn into the kingdom of God. Therefore, our worldview, what we think, has been shaped by our culture, significant others, the media, our environment and many other variables; thus making our thinking earthy. In order to gain the heavenly perspective, we must be transformed, by our minds being renewed through the Holy Spirit and knowledge of our Lord and Savior, Jesus Christ (see Romans 12:1, 2). 2 Peter 1:3 promises that, Christ has given to us all things that pertain to living a godly life, through the knowledge of Him. God's call is to His kingdom and glory (see Matthew 6:33); 1 Thessalonians 2:12; 2 Thessalonians 2:13-14); to life eternal (1 Timothy 6:12); and to His marvelous light (1 Peter 2:9).

This is a universal call to all men in its application and demands a universal proclamation through means other than the Word in the Scriptures, namely man's consciousness of the creation (see Romans 1:18-20), and a direct call through the preaching of the gospel. The former is inadequate without the latter; therefore, the church is required to go into the entire world and preach the gospel to every creature.

The Absolute Need for the Messenger
How shall they call on Him whom they have not believed? And how shall they believe in Him whom they have not heard? And how shall they hear without a preacher? (Romans 10:14). Paul asks, "How shall they hear without a preacher?" (v.14). He does not mean that all of us must enter public

ministry to preach the gospel. The Greek word used for preacher here, defines one who heralds, proclaims, or publishes. Clearly, every believer is assigned a personal pulpit in the home, community, the work place, school, while shopping or during appointments from which to show and tell others the Good News, and don't forget, not without the blood of Christ. Behold the Man! Don't miss the privilege of sharing this Good News. We must not get so busy that we don't tell our neighbors. Get busy telling! When God says go, He means now! Many local churches and individual believers lack vision; therefore millions will be lost (see Proverbs 29:18). What's your vision for lost souls?

Luke 19:10 gives us our Lord's mission, *"for the Son of man has come to seek and to save that which was lost."* He is our example; therefore, His mission is our mission. The early church had a fiery passion for souls. In Romans 1:14 Paul declares, *"I am a debtor,"* very pointedly noting his sense of obligation. Why? He answers in Ephesians 2: Man is dead, needing life (v.1), man is walking a course of destruction, needing deliverance (v.12), man is separated from God, needing Christ (v.14); also see (John 3:16; Acts 10:34). It is by the grace of God through the preaching of the gospel that the call comes to men (see Galatians1:15; 2 Thessalonians 2:14). Be grateful!

Receiving and Understanding

The preacher must study, be trained, and possess a clear understanding that the message is his or her responsibility. Jesus, Himself concludes the evidence of man's need: He is lost, needing to be found (see Luke 19:10). Here is the answer, someone must be sent to preach so that people hear, understand and believe. There is no other way (see Romans 3:23; 2 Corinthians 10:15-16).

The gospel will meet with varying degrees of understanding in the human heart. In Matthew 13:1-20, Jesus illustrated this truth in the parable of the sower. The gospel being the Word of God (seed) sown by the sower into the field (hearts of men). Understanding of the gospel sown brought forth a harvest as determined by the condition of the ground (heart) into which it was sown. Four different degrees of understanding are depicted in the parable. The hearts (grounds) depicted here are hard, stony, thorny and good:

- The hard heart hears the Word, but does not understand the gospel seed, so Satan comes and snatches away that which was sown into his or her heart. This one received the seed by the wayside. Like the roadside, this heart is packed hard due to heavy traffic (v.19).

- The stony heart receives the Word with joy, yet he or she has no roots or depth within to sustain it. When tribulation or persecution comes because of the Word this person immediately stumbles (vv. 20-21).

- The thorny heart receives the Word (seed), but the cares of the world and in the case of America today, secularism and materialism choke the Word and this person becomes unfruitful (v.22). An example of this person is one who watches the news religiously, but spends very little time in the Word of God or the things of God. As a result he or she must seek familiar world solutions, rather than trust God, because they lack biblical revelation. This individual is the one who observes or measures the Word of God through their circumstances; instead of seeing their circumstances through the Word of God.

- The good ground (heart) hears the Word understands it and bears fruit which others eat to live (see Galatians 5:22-23), thus producing some a hundredfold, some sixty-fold, some thirty-fold harvests.

Jesus concludes the evidence of man's need, he is lost and needing to be found (see Luke 19:10). Central also in this passage is the fact that Satan has his sowers in the field of the world also (v.25). The Scripture tells us that when the grain sprouted and grew up, the tares (Satan's crop) also appeared. In the sprouting and even the growth stage, the lord of the harvest allows them to grow together because they look similar. Uprooting the tares would uproot and damage some of the wheat sprouts. They continue in this state until the head is formed. Sometime ago, I read the comments of an old experienced Midwestern farmer concerning how we can distinguish the wheat from the tares. He said, "When they are mature and bear fruit, you can tell the wheat because the stem bends or bows due to the weight of its head. The tares grow tall and proud because it has no head (fruit) to weigh it down, so the stiff-necked tares are very visible (vv. 26-30).

In looking at these parables, we can understand the few fruitful laborers in many of our churches and ministries. In the parable of the sower, only one quarter of the listeners was fruitful. Those of us who communicate the gospel weekly as well as those who share the Word of God daily in counsel, witnessing, and conversation should take note. Many times this condition comes as a result of the hearer not clearly understanding the Word sown into their hearts. Additionally, most preachers will admit that 90% or more of preaching is aimed at getting the hearers to do better, while only about 10% is aimed at building up their faith by trusting God. This shows that a majority of preachers think the primary goal of preaching is moral reform. I am convinced that this "do better" or other "self help" theology accomplishes little except leaving the hearers empty and it adds to the confusion and misunderstanding as in the parable of the sower above.

Every sermon should address real-life experience in terms of the sufficiency of God for every need.

We must remain vigilant and relevant preaching in the trust God mode; which actually helps the hearers to grow in their Christian life. Like the men of Issachar, we must understand our times so that we know how to communicate well and reach people (see 1 Chronicles 12:32).

Faith comes by hearing

Remember, the Scripture explains, faith comes by hearing. Hearing is a verb carrying with it the necessity of taking action in order to be activated. So a person's faith comes by what they hear. Our culture is a swirling tornado of media and messages, moving so quickly that multiple interpretations leave the people with no transcendent knobs on which to hang their hearts and souls. We should speak the truth of God's Word in love only after much prayer and preparation. Our personal opinions are useless in this matter. Only truth will prevail.

Two observations should be made before closing this topic:

1. It is the intention of God that all men should hear the gospel; therefore it is the church's obligation to make disciples by bringing individuals to spiritual maturity, through love and diligent biblical doctrinal teaching and obedience of the Great Commandment and the Great Commission respectively:

You shall love the Lord your God with all your heart, with all your soul, and your entire mind. And you shall love your neighbor as yourself (see Matthew 22:37-39).

And Jesus came and spoke to them, saying, "All authority has been given to Me in heaven and on earth. Go therefore and make disciples of all the nations, baptizing them in the name of the Father and of the Son and of the Holy Spirit, teaching them to observe all things that I have commanded you; and lo I am with you always, even to the end of the age, Amen (Matthew 28:18-20). The apostle Paul adds: *And the things that you have heard from me among many witnesses, commit these to faithful men who will be able to teach others also (2 timothy 2:2).*

"Commit" means *"deposit"* and refers to the treasure of Gospel truth that Paul committed to Timothy (see 1 Timothy 6:20) and which God had first committed to Paul (see 1 Timothy 1:11). God has deposited with His people the truth of the Word of God. It is our responsibility to guard it and pass it on to others. The task of the local church today is not to turn inward with the truth; but live it and teach it to future generations. Please note that Paul is to deposit the truth with *"faithful men"* and not just any believer. Faithful men are Spirit-filled, Spirit-led men and women who believes in Christ and in the Word of God. They are loyal, reliable, dependable, trustworthy, fruitful and heeds Paul's exhortation to be diligent in study to show themselves approved unto God workers, who need not be ashamed, rightly dividing the Word of Truth (see 2 Timothy 2:15).

Each passing day more and more of our culture buys into the deceptive lie that truth is relative. Relative means it is determined by the individual or their particular culture. This philosophy born in academia is taught in our schools and found at all levels of our society and has even found expression in our government. The local church is not spared as Christ, the Bible, all that pertain to God, and the things of God are being removed from their rightful place. Many American communities along with their churches are becoming complacent, more religious, but Christ-less (see Revelation 3:14-22). Bibles are not only banned from schools, but also from many local churches; as entertainment replaces the worship and Bible study falls by the wayside. This condition is creating a vacuum which is being quickly filled by new religions and cultic practices. They all come along claiming that there are many ways to God. This is error. *Jesus said, "I am the way, the truth, and the life" (John 14:6).* As was stated earlier in this chapter, God went through great lengths to establish the fact that Jesus is the way, the *only* Way. 1500 years of lessons in the tabernacle proves that *without blood there is no remission of sins (See Hebrews 9:22- 28; 2 Corinthians 5:17, 21) nor impartation of eternal life.* The truth of God and of salvation is established forever. Christ came to earth to reveal God and the *way of salvation.* Considering the various religions claiming other ways can be overshadowed by true Christian living. Since Christianity is contagious, being authentic we can pass it to many. As the apostle Paul so vividly expressed, we are epistles read of men. Will the authentic salt and light please standup! I believe that we have as greater opportunity than even the early church; perhaps because we can read God's Word and therefore receive revelation through the Holy Spirit who lives within us. Truly, our world is without excuse! Hebrews 4:12 tells us, *the Word of God is living and powerful, and sharper than any two-edged sword, piercing even to the division of soul and spirit, and of joints and marrow, and is a discerner of the thoughts and intents of the heart.* As we observe this passage, we can see how imperative it is that we speak the anointed Word of God. Our preaching, teaching, witnessing, biblical counseling and even our conversations demand it. The Bible promises no power in my opinions or your opinions; however, the Word of God does separate man's soul (which comprises his will, mind, and emotions) from his spirit. I believe that when we speak the truth in love, it is God's Word being planted right into the spirits and hearts of men.

Be prayerful in your witness, seek good ground in which to sow (see 2 Timothy 2:2), always being aware of the stony, thorny and hard ground around you. God said that His Word that goes forth from His mouth; would not return to Him void, but accomplish what He pleases (see Isaiah 55:11). The Holy Bible is from the mouth of God; brothers and sisters that Word goes forth through our spirit. Believe that God always finishes what He begins, including His work in you (see Philippians 1:6-7). That planted Word works from the inside out renewing our soul and body. Make loving and knowing Christ your main goal in life. The word, knowing, requires a relationship, and a relationship results in intimacy; which produces a birthing. Mature disciples are prepared to more effectively evangelize the world and to edify the body. Advanced teaching and training through the Word and the Holy Spirit enables the mature Christian to discern the hearts of men and women because they have the mind of Christ (See Hebrews 5:14).

2. Another observation is this, although the gospel call is genuine and produces an intended effect it is not compulsive. The call to salvation is an invitation, not an irresistible demand. We must solemnly remember, the grace of God may be resisted. Discernment, prayer, wisdom, and timing are crucial in all of our endeavors for Christ. God is almighty and man's freedom is limited, but God has given man the freedom to choose (free-will). If this is not true, then man is not responsible for moral choices and God is the only real Person in the universe. Jesus weeping over Jerusalem is an example, *O Jerusalem, Jerusalem, the one who kills prophets and stones those who are sent to her! How often I wanted to gather your children together, as a hen gathers her chicks under her wings, but you were not wiling (Matthew 23:37).* They have rejected the King of glory, and so He leaves them to their own desires. Let me say here, many Scriptures would be rendered meaningless unless it be realized that people may reject the grace of God to his or her own ruin.

Personal Journal Notes

(Reflection & Response)

1. The most important thing that I learned from this chapter was:

2. The area that I need to work on the most is:

3. I can apply this lesson to my life by:

4. Closing Statement of Commitment

❧

Section II
Behold The Man

CHAPTER 5

Jesus Christ: The Promise Fulfilled

S o the LORD God said to the serpent; because you have done this, you are cursed more than all cattle, and more than every beast of the field; on your belly you shall go, and you shall eat dust all the days of your life (Genesis 3:14).

The Promise:

"And I will put enmity between you and the woman, and between your seed and her Seed; He shall bruise your head, and you shall bruise His heel" *(Genesis 3:15).* Though all of creation was cursed as a result of Adam and Eve's disobedience; the physical serpent deserved special mention being made to slither on its belly. In verse 15, God cursed the spiritual serpent, Satan (see Romans 8:20-23; cf. Jeremiah 12:4).

The ruin of the human race had been accomplished by Satan. We see the fruit of Adam's sin when God calls for him in the Garden. Determining themselves, to be naked, they took it upon themselves to determine what was acceptable to God in such a state. So "fig leaf" or "another way" religion was born and still thrives today. The prophetic struggle was on between *your seed* (Satan and unbelievers, also called his children in John 8:44) and *her Seed* (Christ a descendent of Eve and those in Him) began in the Garden. In the first man, Adam, all had died.

In this passage, we also see hope and mercy shone forth. The offspring of the woman called "He" is Christ, who will one day defeat the serpent. Satan could only bruise Christ's heel (cause Him to suffer), while Christ will bruise Satan's head (destroy him with a fatal blow). As stated in an earlier chapter, Genesis 3:21, reveals the first shedding of blood, the first type of mercy and atonement; wherein God killed animals to clothe Adam and Eve, who are now sinners, with coats of skin to cover their nakedness.

The Coming Savior

The coming Savior must be the seed of the woman. A man would understand man and be able to walk with him. On man's side, such a Savior could be trusted. On God's side such a Savior would be fit to substitute to bear the sins of all mankind.

Fast-forward now. Jesus said, "Abraham saw my day and was glad." To Abraham and his seed were the promises given and that holy Seed, who should with Abraham inherit the land of Canaan forever, must be a man who would come from the loins of Abraham, descended through Isaac. The Christ must be of Abraham's linage.

The coming Man was promised to David as his seed, in II Samuel 7:10-16, and in Psalm 89. In other passages the Lord promised David that in the future his throne at Jerusalem would be established forever to his seed. The coming King must be the seed of David, that is, literally a descendent of his and therefore a man.

God revealed to Isaiah that a virgin would conceive and bring forth a Son, Immanuel, God with us (see Isaiah 7:14). Further, He said, *"Unto us a Child is born, unto us a Son is given, and the government will be upon His shoulder. And His name will be called Wonderful, Counselor, Mighty God, Everlasting Father, Prince of Peace" (Isaiah 9:6).* It was Isaiah, too, to whom was revealed the coming Savior as a Man of sorrows, and acquainted with grief." Even to Mary, the angel Gabriel said, *"And behold, you will conceive in your womb and bring forth a Son, and shall call His name Jesus" (Luke 1:31).*

Christ Born of a Virgin

Jesus was born of a virgin. He came into the world the same way as every other human being on earth, except Adam and Eve who were made straight from the hand of God. The Creator of the universe was formed and born with no human father, through the body of a woman. He nursed at a mother's breast, learned from a mother's tongue, and was led by a mother's hand. Babyhood is not the mark of a God but the mark of a man. A God could not be ignorant as a baby without becoming a man. The Son of God has become a man for the love of men, to make a perfect example, to atone for men, to suffer and die for men, and to mediate between God and men.

Little is said of Jesus' childhood; but much is given to emphasize His perfect humanity. The Scripture says that Jesus *"grew in wisdom, stature, and in favor with God and man" (Luke 2:52).* When Christ was born of a virgin, He emptied Himself of His wisdom and chose to be ignorant as a baby so that He like other men could grow in wisdom. In His self-emptying He gave up the glory, the outshining majesty and outward expression of the Godhead that He had with the Father (see John 17:5). He laid aside everything that would give Him an unfair advantage over other men and entered the human race. Often, I've heard men preach that Jesus was rich, they exclaim, how else could He spend three and a half years leading twelve unprofessional men.

However, if Jesus had been materially rich that would have given Him an unfair advantage over other men. He was the perfect example for all men; because this made Him totally dependent upon His Father, God. Certainly it would follow that likewise we must be totally dependent upon Him. We will discuss self-emptying in more detail in a later segment. Christ won, without sin, where no one else ever did and grew in favor with God. He said, *"I do always those things that please Him" (John 8:29).* The Father said at His baptism, *"I am well pleased."*

We know that, Jesus grew and was subject to His mother and foster father. That He was as human as any other child born. He did not sin, and He had an aptitude for spiritual things. But His sinless virtue and anxiety to be about His Father's business were not simply characteristics that He brought into the world. Rather they were His own deliberate choices as a human being. A perfect and sinless human being the only one that ever existed after the Garden of Eden; but yet a human being.

The Necessity of the Virgin Birth

There are two major things which necessitated the virgin birth or incarnation: First was the fall and sinfulness of man, and secondly, the covenant-making and keeping God. This means that as a covenant-keeper, God as the Creator is obligated for the creature (see Genesis 1:26-28). When man sinned God remained obligated by His own will to man, especially in the area of redemption. This is to be fulfilled by the new covenant (see Jeremiah 31:31-34). To state it more explicitly, man sinned and therefore came under the death penalty (see Genesis 2:16-17). He thus needed someone to redeem him from death. However, all those who would be born of Adam's race would be born in sin and need redemption from sin for themselves. None of Adam's race could by any means redeem man (see Psalm 49:7-8; 51:5; 58:3). If man is to be redeemed, then a man must die for man, and since no one from Adam's race qualified, then only God could redeem man, but by His own law, God could not redeem man as God, *He had to become Man.* The fall of man necessitated the covenant-keeping God becoming man in order to redeem man back into relationship with Himself.

It was sin that necessitated the incarnation. However, if God was to become man, it must be without or apart from sin. Otherwise, He Himself would be a sinner unable to save others. God's answer was seen in the virgin birth, in which God clothed Himself with human flesh, and was born of Mary into the human race. But He *did not inherit a fallen, sinful or corrupt nature.* He took *sinless* human nature and united it with the *divine* nature.

When God foretold through the mouth of the prophet Jeremiah that the days would come when He would make a new covenant with the House of Israel and House of Judah, *He obligated Himself to die.* This also necessitated the incarnation, for God could not die as God, but *only* as man (see Jeremiah 31:31-34; also Hebrews 8:8-13; 9:15-17; Matthew 26:26-28). A testament or covenant is only of force after men are dead. Thus the New Covenant or New Testament could not come into effect until after the death of the Testator, Jesus Christ.

The Nature of the Incarnation

The nature of the incarnation is given to us by Paul in the epistle to the Philippians in the seven-fold humiliation of the Christ. The seven steps of Christ's humiliation or self-emptying are as follows in Philippians 2:6-8:

- *Who being in the form of God*

- *Thought it not robbery to be equal with God*

- *But made Him of no reputation*

- *And took upon Himself the form of a servant*

- *And was made in the likeness of men*

- *And being found in the fashion as a man, He humbled Himself*

- *And became obedient unto death, even the death of the cross (vv. 6-8).*

As the God-Man, Jesus never ceased to possess all the attributes of God. He was conscious of His deity as well as His humanity. Because of Christ's sinlessness, His human nature was immortal. All men must die as a result of sin. *The wages of sin is death (Romans 6:23).* Christ having no sin of His own, and conquering every temptation to sin, did not have to die. Sickness, disease or age could not have conquered Him. This makes His death unique, as was His birth and life. Jesus was sinless and therefore immortal.

He voluntarily laid down His life for us. He died for our sins (see John 10:18; 19:30; Romans 5:12-21). No sinful or mortal man could do this. Jesus was immortal because He was sinless; sinless because He was virgin born; and virgin born because He was God incarnate. Being the sinless God-Man He was the perfect revelation of God to man, and the perfect Mediator between God and man. Behold the Man!

Personal Journal Notes
(Reflection & Response)

1. The most important thing that I learned from this chapter was:

2. The area that I need to work on the most was:

3. I can apply this lesson to my life by:

4. Closing Statement of Commitment

CHAPTER 6

Jesus Christ: The Man in the Middle

"*To Jesus the Mediator of the new covenant, and to the blood of sprinkling that speaks better things than that of Abel*" *(Hebrews 12:24). "There is one God and one Mediator between God and men, the Man Christ Jesus" (1Timothy 2:5).*

The word mediator means, a go between, a middle man, a reconciler or one that stands between two parties at variance for the purpose of reconciling them. The New Testament brings into full revelation, in the person of Jesus Christ, that which was shadowed in the Old Testament mediatorial ministry.

The New Covenant Mediator
As our New Covenant, Jesus Christ's mediatorial ministry far surpasses all that was typified in the Old Covenant mediators.

A Sinless Mediator
Christ was a sinless Mediator. He is indeed better than Moses and Aaron who needed redemption (see Hebrews 5:1-5; 8:1-4; 10:1-11).

A Divine-Human Mediator

Jesus Christ was the God-Man. He was God, having the nature of God, thus identifying with God and His absolute holiness. He also became man, taking sinless humanity upon Him and thus identifying with man. This union of the divine and human natures in the one person of Christ qualifies Him to be a perfect mediator between God and man. The Scripture says, *Therefore, in all things He had to be made like His brethren, that He might be merciful and faithful High Priest in things pertaining to God, to make propitiation for the sins of the people (Hebrews 2:17).*

A Union of Deity and Humanity

The Scripture reveals clearly the union of deity and humanity in the one person of Jesus Christ. The union was the union of God and man in one Person, forming the *"new creation"*. Man did not become God but God became Man. *These things says the Amen, the Faithful and True Witness, the Beginning of the creation of God (Revelation 3:14).* Thus Christ has two wills, two distinct natures, in a human and a divine, each of which has its own essential attributes, functions and activities; but both natures belong to the same Person. Christ was begotten of the Father from eternity according to His divine nature (see Psalm 2:7). He was born of the Virgin Mary in the fullness of time according to His human nature (Galatians 4:4). Jesus was 30 years old according to His human nature (Luke 3:23); and according to His divine nature He could say "Before Abraham was, I am" (John 8:58). Christ was equal to the Father as touching His Godhead and He was inferior to the Father as touching His manhood.

Reasons for the Union

The union constitutes Christ as the only perfect Mediator between God and man, between a holy God and a sinful man. Jesus Christ is the *bridge* between God and man. He can stand with God above and with man below. He being the Son of Man (humanity) and the Son of God (deity) thus became "Jacob's Ladder" bridging the gulf between God and man, and heaven and earth; that was brought about through sin. On the cross it was the divine nature offering the sinless human nature to God for sin. It was deity presenting sinless humanity to God as a perfect sacrifice for sin. It was God atoning to God. It was a sinless Man atoning for sinful man. Only the miracle of the incarnation and the union of the two natures in one person made this possible.

If we over-emphasize His deity, we obscure His perfect humanity. If we over-emphasize His humanity, we obscure His deity. If we deny His deity, there is no contact between God and man and the bridge is broken down from the divine side. On the other hand, if we deny His humanity, then the bridge is broken down on the human side. It is the blessed Son of Man, truly Christ, the God-Man the better Mediator of a better covenant.

Personal Journal Notes
(Reflection & Response)

1. The most important thing that I learned from this chapter was:

2. The area that I need to work on the most is:

3. I can apply this lesson to my life by:

4. Closing Statement of Commitment

CHAPTER 7

Jesus Christ: Our Example

As a perfect man, being all that God intended man to be, Christ was totally dependent upon the Father, for all He was, for all He said, and all He did. Christ was the perfect *example* for all believers to follow. The apostle Peter declared that Christ left *us an example that you should follow in His steps (see 1 Peter2:21).*

The Greek word used here is translated *example* means *an underwriting, or copy for imitation.* He only is the *copy* for imitation. All other saints of the Old and New Testament have various character qualities which we may imitate but the best of them have had their imperfections. Christ alone is the perfect copy and He is the only one whom God has set forth for us to *fully* follow. We can follow others as they follow Christ, but when they fail to follow Christ we must cease to follow them (see 1 Corinthians 11:1; Philippians 3:17; 1 John 2:6; Matthew 11:28-30).

It is *impossible* for unregenerate men to imitate Christ. Why? Because of a word that Christianity gave new meaning, *love.* The Greek word agape (love) denotes and undefeatable goodwill and benevolence that always seeks the highest good of the other person, no matter what he or she does. It is the self-giving love that gives freely without asking anything in return, and does not consider the worth of its object. Agape is more a love by choice than philos, which is love by chance; and it refers to the will rather than the emotion. Agape describes the unconditional love God has for the world (see John 3:16). Paul tells us in Romans 5:5 that this is the love of God that has been poured out in our hearts by the Holy Spirit who was given to us. The believer receives the Holy Spirit in new birth and becomes a partaker of the divine nature thus enabling him or her to imitate Christ and follow in the steps of His example. The world needs to see Christ's example in our daily lives; they will know we are Christians by our agape (love).

As the Church of God, we should constantly remind ourselves of this truth. Christ is our only example! Not some athlete, Hollywood star or other famous world figures most of who have never met the Christ of God. What then is the example set forth in Christ's perfect Manhood in which steps we are to imitate and follow?

He is our Example in Character – All He Was
The moral character and qualities of God were manifested in Christ as the perfect Man. These moral attributes *are to be manifested* in the believer also; as he or she is transformed to the image of Christ. I will list several of the main character qualities which are to be in the believer:

Holiness
Jesus is our Example in holiness. He was holy in nature and conduct. The apostle Peter admonishes us, *"but as He who called you is holy, you also be holy in all your conduct, because it is written, "Be holy for I am holy."* He is the example of sinless perfection and it is to this goal that God intends to ultimately bring His people (see Matthew 5:48; Hebrews 6:1; Luke 1:35; Acts 2:37; 3:14; 4:27; Hebrews 7:26; 1 Peter 2:21-23; John 8:29, 46; 14:30; Hebrews 4:15). The person committed to God's holiness says, No! to fleshly lusts and lives for the will of God. The holy person is always alert, keeping

his or her mind clear, and fit for their walk with God. Be honest, sincere, and pure in all your relationships. Love one another fervently!

Love

As I stated above, Christ is our Example in love, which is the very nature of God and to be revealed in the saints. *To know the love of Christ which passes knowledge; that you may be filled with all the fullness of God (Ephesians 3:19).*

- He loved the Father God (John 14:31; 6:38).

- He loved the Scriptures (Matthew 5:17-18; Luke 4:16-21; 24:44-45; John 10:34-36).

- He loved His own disciples (John 13:1; 15:9; Romans 8:37-39).

- He loves the church as His own bride (Ephesians 5:25-27).

- He loves all men regardless of race (Mark 10:21; Matthew 11:19; John 10:11; 15:13; Romans 5:8).

- He loved even His enemies (Matthew 5:43-48; Luke 22:51; 23:34; Matthew 26:50).

- He prayed that this love would be in us (John 17:26; 13:34-35).

- He was continually moved with compassion towards others (John 11:35; 6:5; Mark 6:34; Matthew 8:16; 20:34; Luke 4:41; 5:12-15).

Faith

Christ is our example in faith. He trusted in His Father continually and never doubted; listen to the testimonies of His enemies:

- He saved others (Matthew 27:42; Acts 10:38).

- He trusted in God (v.43; Psalm 22:8).

Oh! What would our churches be like; if this could be said of all Christians? Christ is our only example. We are to look unto Him, *the author and finisher of our faith* (see Hebrews 12:1-4).

Humility

Christ is our example in humility. No pride, no harshness, nor arrogance ever manifested themselves in Him. In the Gospel of John, Jesus' life becomes open to us. He frequently speaks of His relationship with the Father, of the motives by which He was guided, and of His consciousness of the power and Spirit in which He acts. While the word humble is not written, His humility is clearly revealed. Humility defined is nothing but the Christian simply consenting to let God be all, and he or she surrendering totally to His working alone.

In Christ we see Him both as the Son of God in heaven, and as the Son of Man on earth. He totally subordinated Himself. He gave God the honor and glory which is due Him. And what He taught often was made true to Himself: *"He who humbles himself will be exalted (Luke 18:14).* As it is written, *"He humbled Himself wherefore God also has highly exalted Him"* *(Philippians 2:8-9).*

When Christ speaks of His relationship to His Father, He uses the words *not* and *nothing,* of Himself. The *not I,* in which Paul expresses his relationship to Christ, is the very spirit of what Christ says of His relationship to the Father. *"The Son can do nothing of Himself"* *(John 5:19).* *"I can of My own self do nothing; My judgment is just, because I do not seek My own will"* *(John 5:30).* *"I receive not honor from men"* *(John 5:41).* *"I *came down from heaven, not to do Mine own will" (John 6:38). "Neither came I myself, but He sent Me" (John 8:42). "The words that I speak unto you, I speak not from Myself" (John 14:10). "The word which you hear is not Mine but the Father's who sent Me" (John 14:24).*

These words tell us how the Almighty God was able to work His mighty redemptive work through Christ. They show how important Christ counted the state of the heart which became Him as the Son of Man. Christ found this life of entire self-renunciation, of absolute submission and dependence upon the Father's will, to be one of perfect peace and joy. He lost nothing by giving everything to God. The Father honored His trust and did all for Him, and then exalted Him to His right hand in glory.

And because Christ had thus humbled Himself before God and God was ever before Him, He found it possible to humble Himself before men too. He was able to be the Servant of all. His humility was simply the surrender of Himself to God, to allow the Father to do in Him what He pleased, no matter what men might say of Him or do to Him.

This is the true self-denial to which our Savior calls us, the acknowledgment that self has nothing good in it *except* as an empty vessel which God must fill. Jesus teaches us that true humility takes its rise and finds its strength in the knowledge that it is God who works all in all, that our place is to yield to Him in perfect resignation and dependence, in full consent to be and to do nothing of ourselves. This is the life Christ came to reveal and impart to us, a life in God that comes through death to sin and to self. How can I die to self? First of all it is not just something that I do; but it is a work that God does in me.

The Scriptures says, *"Or do you not know that as many of us as were baptized into His death? Likewise you also reckon yourselves to be dead indeed to sin, but alive to God in Christ Jesus, our Lord. And do not present your members as instruments of unrighteousness to sin, but present yourselves to God as being alive from the dead, and your members as instruments of righteousness to God" (Romans 6:3, 11, 13).* Christ lives this life in us through His indwelling Spirit.

For if when we were enemies we were reconciled to God through the death of His Son, much more, shall be saved by His life (Romans 5:10). If while we were yet the enemies of God, Christ was able to reconcile us through His death, certainly He can keep us by His resurrection power. We are further told that we are to adopt Christ's attitude of humility, meekness, unselfishness, servanthood, obedience and let the mind of Christ be in us, believers (see Philippians 2:5-8; Matthew 11:28-30; II Corinthians 10:1).

Word

Christ is the perfect example of all that He said. The words He spoke were His Father's words.

a.   Christ is our example in what He said, *"For I have not spoken of My own authority; but the Father who sent Me gave Me a command, what I should say and what I should speak" (John 12:49).*

b.   He is our example in prayer life. If the Son of Man depended on prayer to maintain communication with the Father, how much more should the believer (See Hebrews 5:7; Luke 6:12; Matthew 14:23; Mark 1:35-38; John 11:41-42; John 17).

c.   He is our example in preaching and teaching (See Matthew 23:8; John 3:2; 7:16; Matthew 7:29; 11:28-29).

Deed

Christ is our example in all that He did. He worked in secular life as a carpenter and His Messianic work, doing His Father's will. He went about doing good. Jesus was a man of deeds as well as words. He fully obeyed the Father's will (See Acts 1:1; John 6:38; Matthew 26:39; Psalm 40:8; John 4:31-34; 5:30).

Personal Journal Notes

(Reflection & Response)

1. The most important thing that I learned from this chapter was:

2. The area that I need to work on the most is:

3. I can apply this lesson to my life by:

4. Closing Statement of Commitment

OUR

DUAL PROBLEM: SINS & SIN

&

DUAL REMEDIES

CHAPTER 8

Remedy: The Blood of Jesus Christ

J n all His dealings with us, God works by taking us out of the way and substituting Christ in our place. The Son of God died instead of us for our forgiveness. He lives instead of us for our deliverance. So, we have two substitutions introduced here to solve our dual problems of sins and sin.

I will take as a starting point the view of these two substitutions as the Holy Spirit revealed though the apostle Paul in the first eight chapters of the Book of Romans. Many call the Book of Romans the fifth Gospel. The reason is obvious when we notice the natural division of the first eight chapters. There is a striking difference in the subject matter of its two parts. The four and a half chapters from 1:1 to 5:11 form the first division and 5:12 to 8:39 form the second division. A very noticeable difference, in the first division we find the plural word, sins emphasized. In the second the singular word, sin is prominent.

Why the Difference?

We can illustrate this by looking at *sin* as the factory and *sins* as the product produced by the factory. God concerns Himself not only with our sins but He is concerned with destroying the factory, sin. It is a question of the sins I have committed before God and then secondly, it is a question of a sin principle working in me. No matter how many sins I commit, it is always the one sin principle within me that produces the sins. Therefore, I need forgiveness for my sins, but I also need deliverance from the power of sin.

The Problem of our Sins

We begin with the precious blood of Jesus and its value for us in dealing with our sins and justifying us in the sight of God. Notice the following passages: *"All have sinned" (Romans 3:23)*. *"But God demonstrated His own love toward us, in that while we were still sinners, Christ died for us. Much more then, having now been justified by His blood, we shall be saved from wrath through Him" (Romans 5:8, 9)*. *"Being justified freely by His grace through the redemption that is in Christ Jesus, whom God set forth as a propitiation by His blood, through faith, to demonstrate His righteousness, because in His forbearance God had passed over the sins that were previously committed, to demonstrate at the present time His righteousness, but He might be just and the justifier of the one who has faith in Jesus" (Romans 3:24-26)*.

In the first part of Romans, chapters 1 – 8, twice we have reference to the blood of the Lord Jesus, in chapter 3:25 and in chapter 5:9. The argument here centers on the aspect of Jesus' work which is represented by His blood shed for our justification through the remission of sins. We see then, the blood deals with what we have done; which is a marked difference than the second division which we shall see in the next chapter deals with the Cross and what we are.

The Solution to Sins

As stated in earlier chapters, sin came about as a result of Adam's choice; which resulted in an act of disobedience to God (see Romans 5:19). This disobedience created a separation between God and man. God can no longer have fellowship with him, for there is something now that hinders and gives man a sense of guilt. Our sins had first to be dealt with, and this was done by the precious blood of Jesus Christ and at the same time the blood of Christ cleanses our conscience (See Ephesians 2:6; Hebrews 10:19-23).

Knowing that you were not redeemed with corruptible things, like silver or gold, from your aimless conduct received by tradition from your fathers, but with the precious blood of Christ, as of a lamb without blemish and without spot (1 Peter 1:18-19). The blood of Jesus Christ is the price of our purchase or redemption. God offers Christ's blood to us as our substitution sacrifice and accepts it when we offer it back to Him. Our transaction with God is therefore not a gold and silver economy, but a life and death economy. Christ gave His life's blood to buy us out of sin and death. Our valuation of the blood of Jesus is only according to God's valuation. I come to God on the finished work of the Man, Jesus. I approach God through His merit alone, and never on the basis of my attainment; never, for example, on the ground that I have been extra kind or patient today, or that I have done something for the Lord this morning. I have to come by way of the blood every time, not my performance. God looks on the blood of the Son of Man and He is satisfied.

Entering His Presence

When Jesus died the Scripture tells us that the veil (the thick curtain between the holy place and the holy of holies (see Hebrews 6:19; 9:3; 10:20) in the temple ripped from top to bottom indicating that this was not an act of mere man; but of the Son of Man, Jesus. His death opened the way into the presence of God (see Matthew 27:51). God's acceptance of the blood is the ground upon which we may come boldly to the throne of grace that we may obtain mercy and find grace to help in time of need (see Hebrews 4:16). Behold the Man!

As with many other facts of our Christian experience, entering God's presence has two phases, the initial phase and the progressive phase:

- *The initial Phase*

Our standing with God was secured by the blood of Christ, *even when we were dead in trespasses, made us alive together with Christ (by grace you have been saved), and raised up together, and made us sit together in heavenly places in Christ Jesus (Ephesians 2:5-6).* Notice, the three *"togethers"* in vv. 5 and 6, our union with Christ:

- In His resurrection

- In His ascension

- In His present rule at God's right hand

This phase is illustrated in **(Figure 2)** below:

FIGURE 2

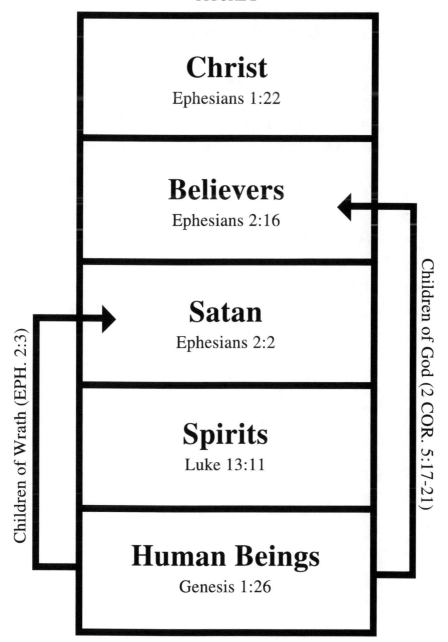

Christt
Ephesians 1:22

Believers
Ephesians 2:16

Satan
Ephesians 2:2

Spirits
Luke 13:11

Human Beings
Genesis 1:26

Children of Wrath (EPH. 2:3)

Children of God (2 COR. 5:17-21)

Jesus Christ is far above all principalities and powers. Notice in Figure 2 above. We are complete in Him and seated with Him in heavenly places, far above all principality and power and might and dominion (see Ephesians 1:20-21). The New Testament reveals an invisible realm of evil powers that deceives and manipulates human behavior thereby advancing Satan's strategies to wreck God's plans for man. Christ Himself and all who are in Him are shown to be positioned above all of these powers, and authorities that only spiritual warfare can assert (offense), demonstrate (example), and sustain (continually). It is worthy of note to point out that we have only one enemy, Satan. Our fellowman is the enemy only to the extent that he or she let Satan use them. *"We do not wrestle against flesh and blood, but against principalities, against powers, against the rulers of the darkness of this age, against spiritual hosts of wickedness in heavenly places* (See Ephesians 6:12). Paul further admonishes, *"Put on the whole armor of God that you may be able to withstand in the evil day, and having done all, to stand" (v. 13)*. Stand in readiness for spiritual combat. Recognize that your demonic enemies are behind much of what comes against you. All of this armor is not just a passive protection in facing the enemy; it is to be used offensively against these satanic forces. Paul was in prison and under constant guard when writing the Ephesus church. Forced to look at the soldier's armor daily he had an ideal picture of the armor needed by the Christian believer to combat the forces of evil. In Ephesians 6:14-17, he lists six pieces of armor essential for each Christian soldier to stand ready:

- Loins girt about with truth (v. 14)

- Breastplate of righteousness (v. 14)

- Feet shod with the preparation of the gospel of peace (v. 15)

- The shield of faith (v. 16)

- The helmet of salvation (v. 17)

- The sword of the Spirit, the Word of God (v. 17)

Notice Paul's final order: We are to be "praying always with all prayer and supplication in the Spirit" (v. 18). While prayer is not a part of the armor; it is the means by which we engage the enemy for prayer is the battle itself, with God's Word being our chief offensive weapon deployed against Satan during the struggle. To see how Christ, our Example, employed this great offensive weapon against Satan (see Matthew 4:1-11).

In Ephesians 1:17-18, Paul prayed that the people of God receive "the spirit of wisdom and revelation" with the dual objective of their knowing Christ and understanding God's power and purpose in their lives. Revelation here refers to an unveiling of our hearts that we may receive:

- Clear perception

- Applicable wisdom

- An understanding of the Word of God

- Clear understanding of God's will for you

- Understand how God intended His Word to work in building our lives.

In the parable of the wise and the foolish builders, Jesus emphasizes the absolute necessity of knowing and doing the will of God; that is, what God has told us to do (see Matthew 7:24-27).

Revelation may be used in preaching and teaching that is especially anointed in helping people see the glory of Christ and His purpose and power in them. The mere mention of such a realm brings laughter and jest among many people in this nation; which very sadly includes many professors in the church. It's so amazing how the god of this world can manipulate Hollywood into making fantasies and terror films about reality that help keep many, even some Christians in unbelief. Satan's deceptions, which are labeled everything except what they truly are sin and demonic activity. They appear under various names as seen daily on TV, one man taking on an uncontrollable disease or enemy from outer space alone, impossible? Yes, but the star always wins. The newspapers and other media carry the story of a dreaded disease with no known cure; people panic and demand a cure; so the officials give the disease a name; the people are soothed as if the name is a cure. The people return to their play. That thing that was a sin forty or fifty years ago is now a disease with an acceptable name. Demonic and sinful behavior has been given an unpronounceable name. Decon is rat poison; and will kill you no matter what name or label you put on it. The wages of sin is still death. It is really satanic deception and demonic forces at work. That is so sad!

- *The progressive phase*

This second phase is our continued access to God. Our continual access remains only by His blood and His High Priest ministry. The writer of Hebrews exhorts us: "Having therefore boldness to enter into the holy place *by the blood* of Jesus Let us draw near" (Hebrews 10:19, 22). We are to hold fast to our confession of our hope without wavering, for He who promised is faithful (v. 23):

Keys to Progressive Access to God

- Give your full attention to God's Word and your relationship with the Man, Jesus.

- Let Jesus and His Word be the foundation and sustainer of all your thinking.

- Praise God daily for your continued access to God through the shed blood of Jesus.

- Continually draw near to God with a blameless heart and faith.

- Fail not to gather with God's people to encourage and urge them on in righteousness.

- Seek God diligently and believe that He will reward your diligence.

- Practice persistent and patient praise.

Personal Journal Notes

(Reflection & Response)

1. The most important thing that I learned from this lesson was:

2. The area that I need to work on the most is:

3. I can apply this lesson to my life by:

4. Closing Statement of Commitment

CHAPTER 9

Remedy: The Cross of Jesus Christ

When we know the precious truth of justification by faith we still know only half of the story, our sins (See for example, Romans 3:24-26; 4:5, 25). We still have only solved the problem of standing before God. As we go on, God has something more to offer us, namely, the remedy for the sin principle; which affects our character and behavior showing what we are.

The corresponding question then, is that of sanctification (See Romans 6:19, 22). So we must move on. The blood can wash away my sins but it cannot wash away the sin principle in me. It needs the Cross to crucify me. The blood deals with the sins (products), but the Cross must deal with the sin principle (factory).

There are bad sinners and there are good sinners, there are moral sinners and there are corrupt sinners, but they are all sinners. We sometimes think that if only we had not done certain things all would be well; but the trouble lies deeper than in what we do, it lies in what we are. That is also a fallacy actually promoted in our society, what you can or cannot do (performance) is more important than what you are (character). So your character is secondary just don't rock the boat. The attitude is as long as it doesn't affect production or give the company a bad name. The Lord's interests are not in our abilities, but in our availability.

This performance oriented attitude is very prevalent in many local churches; as some of the people are very gifted, but have allowed their gifts to exceed (or outrun) their character. Satan is very pleased! He knows man after observing him for the past six thousand years. He waits until we are in the right position, then he kicks the stool out from under us exposing who we really are.

Man's State by Nature

We come now to Romans 5:12-21. In this great passage grace is brought into contrast with sin and the obedience of Christ is set against the disobedience of Adam. The Holy Spirit placed it at the beginning of the second division of Romans (5:12 to 8:39) which shall be our focus, and its argument leads to the conclusion of the matter. It is found in verse 19: *"For as through the one man's disobedience the many were made sinners, even so through the obedience of the one shall the many be made righteous."* Here the Holy Spirit is seeking to show us first what we are, and then how it was that we came to be what we are.

At the beginning of our Christian life we are concerned with what we are doing not so much with what we are. We think that if only we could be good and do certain things, go to church every Sunday, tithe, and keep the Commandments every thing will be pleasing to God, so we set out to do it. But soon we notice the results of this living are not what we expected. We discover that it is more than just a case of trouble on the outside; that there is trouble on the inside. We try to please God, but find something within our very being that does not want to please Him. We try to be humble, but there is something within our being that wants to rebel. We try being loving, but there is something within that makes us feel most unloving.

We smile and try to look very gracious, but inwardly we feel decidedly ungracious. The more we try to rectify things on the outside the more we realize how deep-seated our trouble really is. Then reality hits us, and we turn to the Lord and say, "Lord I see it now. Not only what I have done is wrong, I am wrong!"

As I said at the outset the blood washed away my sins, but it can't wash away "my old sin nature." One thing is for sure, every one of us have been in Eden. When Adam sinned, we were right there in him. So, in Adam we receive everything that is of Adam; and likewise, in Christ we receive everything that is of Christ.

Here we are presented with a new possibility. In Adam all was lost. By him sin entered and death through sin; since that day sin has reigned unto death among the human race; but now a ray of light shines on the scene. Through the obedience of another we may be made righteous. Where sin abounded grace did much more abound, and as sin reigned unto death, even so may grace reign through righteousness into eternal life by Jesus Christ our Lord (see Romans 5:19-21).

God's Devine Way of Deliverance
In God's plan of salvation it is very clear, that He intends the very meaning of the word, salvation to include our practical deliverance from sin, as well as our forgiveness for committed sins. The apostle Paul makes this quite clear when he opens chapter 6 of his letter to the Romans with the question: "What shall we say then? Shall we continue in sin that grace may abound? Certainly not! How shall we who died to sin live any longer in it?" (vv.1-2). Paul's whole being recoils at the very suggestion.

The idea of a Christian continuing in sin is entirely contrary to the gospel. Sin is hateful and destructive, and those who have died to the love of sin and its ruling power should never want to live in it any longer. Water baptism is a symbol of our union with Christ in His death, burial, and resurrection (see vv. 4-5; Colossians 3:1).

God has made adequate provision that we should be set free from sin's dominion. Since we know that the blood cannot set us free, what can set us free? There is only one way. Since we came into the world by birth we must go out by death. To do away with sin, the (factory) we must do away with our life. Bondage to sin came by birth; deliverance from sin comes by death and it is just the way of escape that God has provided. Give Him praise! *"We died to sin" (Romans 6:2).*

The question is then, how do we die? Though we tried in our own strength to get rid of this sinful life and failed. It is not by trying to kill ourselves, but it is by recognizing that God has dealt with us in Christ. The apostle's next statement sums it up, *"Or do you not know that as many of us as were baptized into Christ Jesus were baptized into His death?"* Thank God for grace, we all know that it is impossible for us to get into Christ on our own. Again, God has come to our rescue He did it for us. *"But of Him you are in Christ Jesus" (1 Corinthians 1:30).* Give Him praise!

We don't have to plan our way in. God has planned it for us; and He has also performed it. Righteousness is a judicial term. It is God's determination to right every wrong, His gift to the guilty which removes condemnation and puts them in a state of justification, including full acquittal from all charges against them. When the Lord Jesus was on the cross all of us died, not individually for we had not been born yet, but being in Him, we died in Him. "If One died for all then all died" (2 Corinthians 5:14). When He was crucified all of us were crucified there with Him. Thank you Lord! Behold the Man!

The story is told of an old farmer and his two sons. He had made out his will and on his death bed he called the two sons in to let them know their inheritance. To one he willed the old farm and to the other he left his old worn Bible. The young man was so upset that he slammed the Bible on a nearby table. The old man died and the angry young man packing his suitcase looked at the old Bible, packed it also and left home. He declared that he would never return. Through the years he would sometimes point to the old Bible and joke about how his father had cheated him and favored the other son. Some years later as he laid on his own deathbed a hungry, lonely, homeless, vagabond, he picked up the old Bible and opened it for the first time. There he found an old yellowed envelope with his name on it. Inside the envelope were a note and a check for $5,000 dollars. The note read son, "I love you. I know you are not interested in this old farm, so I left it to your brother. With this money I hope you will have a decent start in life." Tears rolled from his eyes as they closed in death.

As I write this I think of the many people, even in the church who treat the Bible that our Heavenly Father has left us; and like this man hate God, our Father, for their miserable lives. Yet never read this love letter nor come to realize the love and the riches He has left them. My friend, you might be one of those who have never tasted the Father's love. Listen to just one verse concerning His love, "For God so loved the world that He gave His only begotten Son, that whoever believes in Him should not perish but have everlasting life" (John 3:16). Our salvation cost Jesus His life (see John 12:24). He is our Example. It also costs us full repentance and the giving of our lives totally to God. If you have not made a decision yet; I pray that you will do so now, for the time is short! As you have probably realized from your reading so for, He has done it all. He left nothing to us except to repent, accept the fact that we are sinners, and turn to Him in faith for our salvation. Won't you do that right now?

We have looked at the first chapter of 1 Corinthians to establish the fact that we are in Christ Jesus. Now we will go to the end of this same letter to see something more of what this means. In 1 Corinthians 15:45, 47 two remarkable names are used for our Lord Jesus Christ. He is spoken of there as the last Adam and He is spoken of too as the second Man. The distinction of the two enshrines a truth of great value.

As the last Adam, Christ is the sum total of humanity; and as the second Man, He is the Head of a new creation. So we have two unions, one relating to His death and the other to His resurrection. In the first place His union with humanity as the last Adam began historically in Bethlehem and ended at Calvary and the tomb. In it He gathered up into Himself all that was in Adam and took it to judgment and death. In the second place our union with Him as the second Man begins in resurrection and ends in eternity; which is to say, it never ends. Praise God! For having in His death done away with the first man in whom God's purpose was derailed, He rose again as Head of a new creation of men, in whom that purpose will at long last be realized. As the last Adam He wiped out the old creation; as the second Man He brings forth a new creation of man. It is in His resurrection that He stands forth as the second Man, and there too we are included. Paul adds, *"For if we have been united together in His death, certainly we also shall be in the likeness of His resurrection" (Romans 6:5).* The cross then is a mighty act of God which translates us from Adam to Christ.

Personal Journal Notes

(Reflection & Response)

1. The most important thing that I learned from this lesson was:

2. The area that I need to work on the most is:

3. I can apply this lesson to my life by:

4. Closing Statement of Commitment

CHAPTER 10

Dead to Sin: Alive to Christ

In chapter 9 we saw how God destroyed the sin principle and delivered us from sin's reign over us through union with Christ in His death. As slaves to sin we produced or committed sins. Born into a sinful world, we developed sinful habits, a secular worldview and strongholds. No matter how good we were the sin principle reigned over us.

Dead to Sin

Jesus Christ came into the world and died in our stead on Calvary. He died to sin and through our union with Him we died also (factory closed). Now we are freed from sin's reign over us. We have to walk in this truth and resist sin; so that sin will not revive in our mortal bodies. Though our union with Christ in His death has delivered us from the dominion of sin; we still find sin struggling to gain the upper hand over us. As a boy I watched my father clear wooded areas for planting. He dynamited the stumps and cleared out the roots. I noticed if he did not go through this process new growth would sprout from the stump or roots. We must be cleansed from the roots of sin.

Regeneration

I explain this fully in Appendix I of my book: *How Should We Then Live?* There I explain how in regeneration the Holy Spirit quickens (make alive) our spirit which was dead as a result of sin. Therefore, making those who receive Christ as their Savior justified before God:

> *"Now to him who works, the wages are not counted as grace but as debt. But to him who does not work but believes on Him who justifies the ungodly, his faith is accounted for righteousness" (Romans 4:4-5).*

Man is a triune being in that we are three in one; which includes spirit, soul, and body (see 1 Thessalonians 5:23). As stated earlier, we were born in sin and our spirits were dead. In this state we were under the control of our soul. Our soul comprises our mind, will, and affection; with our mind being the driving agent of the three. The apostle Paul said it so clearly, *"When I want to do good, evil is right there with me" (see Romans 7:21).* Our soul and body must be renewed. This will be covered under our next subtopic.

The Propensity to Sin

While this propensity or temptation to sin is present, the Holy Spirit who has now taken up residence in our spirit maintains within us a desire to separate ourselves from evil (1 John 3:9). This can be fulfilled however, only as the result of a renewed mind. Paul admonishes us to not allow this world to conform or shape us into its mold; but to be transformed by the renewing of our minds (see Romans 12:1-2). Transformation comes from the Greek word "metamorpho" meaning to "change to something else." Our English word metamorphosis comes from this word. The best example we have of metamorphosis is the butterfly; which has its beginning as a lowly caterpillar crawling upon the earth. At some point this caterpillar is spun into a cocoon wherein it is transformed or changed into something else, a beautiful butterfly. It is no longer a caterpillar crawling on the ground but now a beautiful monarch butterfly soaring up, up in the beautiful sunshine.

I came across a story some time ago about a man walking down the street, as he was walking along he noticed a butterfly struggling to get free of a sack-like cocoon, as he reached to help set it free; a voice behind him screamed, "Don't touch it!" Too late, he had set the butterfly free; it immediately fell to the ground fluttered and died. Confused the young man asked, "What happened?" The lady told him that the struggle the butterfly was going through to free itself was a part of the transformation process wherein its wings and body would develop survival strength. A growth process that is required for the survival of all butterflies. Likewise, in regeneration, after we are justified through the blood of Jesus, we go through a process of transformation or sanctification.

Sanctification

"Therefore, if anyone is in Christ, he is a new creation; old things have passed away; behold all things have become new" (2 Corinthians 5:17).

This process of transformation or change (new creation) in the man or woman in Christ is a part of regeneration known as sanctification. The apostle Paul gives us explicit instructions for sanctification:

"I beseech you therefore, brethren, by the mercies of God, that you present your bodies a living sacrifice, holy, acceptable to God, which is your reasonable service. And do not be conformed to this world, but be transformed by the renewing

*of your mind, that you may prove what is that good and
acceptable and perfect will of God" (Romans 12:1-2).*

Presenting Your Body to God

As you can see the sanctification Paul speaks of in the above passage has
nothing to do with becoming a believer in Christ. Paul is talking about a
two-fold action that follows the decision to become a Christian:

• Present your bodies to God

• A living sacrifice

This second stage of regeneration requires a believer to *separate himself
or herself* from the world and separate to the Lord. Romans 12:1 invites
believers to take this next step; which can happen immediately upon being
born again, or later even years later. However, the later one waits he or she
finds themselves repeatedly floundering in their pursuit of sanctification.

Why must we present our Bodies?

The answer to this question once again demonstrates the incredible grace
of the Lord, Jesus Christ. Realize what is true about you even before you
present your bodies. *"Do you not know that your body is the temple of the
Holy Spirit who is in you, whom you have from God, and you are not your
own? For you are bought at a price; therefore glorify God in your body and in
your spirit, which are God's" (1 Corinthians 6:19-20).*

The Man, Jesus Christ took ownership of your body from the moment
you were born again. His death on Calvary was the price tag for the
purchase of your life. Therefore, you are not your own, but you may
have been living as if you were your own up to this point. Why didn't
Paul choose to tell the entire story; that we are already God's and we had

better live like it? The Lord always seeks the voluntary dedication of His children.

The Decision at the Door

Following Christ requires a personal decision from each person at the outset. Jesus made some very profound statements about Himself, one *"I am the Door."* In essence, He is saying, He is the only way to God. We hear clamoring everywhere about a number of "other ways to God." So, if we are truly His; then we have already settled that issue. His way!

He knows that unless our heart (body, soul, and spirit) are *committed (for life),* our actions will become *uncommitted (sporadic at best).* So, even though you and I already belong to the Lord, He invites us to voluntarily present our bodies, the house that I /you share with the Holy Spirit, to Him. Living sacrifices means abandoning to Him *all rights to myself (my will, my mind, and my emotions).* Because your act of consecration or separation is "my reasonable service," The act of releasing yourself to the Lord should be the most logical and mentally defensible thing you will ever do. We will return to this discussion in a later topic.

The Scriptures explain that all of this is accomplished through the Holy Spirit and the Word of God. Jesus prayed, *"Sanctify them through your truth: your Word is truth" (John 17:17).* Certain definite changes occur in the process. Through the Word our minds are renewed (to the mind of Christ); as all areas of life after the rebirth are to be. This process is totally impossible without the power of the Holy Spirit. Science can alter the mind, but only God can change it. With this renewal, our seat of control moves from our heads to our hearts. We begin to think thoughts after our Source, God. Prior to our rebirth we ran to sins; but after our rebirth we run from sins.

True repentance is undergoing transformation by the renewing of the mind. We hate what God hates. How do we know what displeases God? We study the Bible. Many have been taught that to repent means to turn and go in a different direction. That is true. But the *first step* is to change one's mind about the matter of sin. We must first decide that sin is not worth the cost; not only in our own life, but in future generations. Once we've repented, we must allow our minds to be totally transformed and renewed by the Holy Spirit and the Word of God (see 2 Peter 1:3).

A fierce battle is being waged for our minds. These changes are offensive to the natural mind; which has naturally relied upon logic and reason. It has enjoyed its freedom secured through sin. However, the mind, will, and emotions are now subject to our spirit; which is now indwelt by the Holy Spirit. God is seeking to transform us to attain our place in Christ. The enemy is trying all forms of bondage to keep us from having an effective relationship with God. Thus, we see that allowing our minds to be transformed by God does require warfare. We must learn, therefore, how to resist the devil in our minds and hearts. We have already stressed the importance of knowing the Scriptures, Peter admonishes us to "Grow in grace and the knowledge of our Lord and Savoir, Jesus Christ" (see 2 Peter 3:18). The Scriptures are the key not only to resisting the devil, but also in transforming our minds to the mind of Christ. As we cultivate a deeper relationship with our Lord, He will bring healing to our minds and hearts however, we must fight the battle of persistence in our relationship with Christ by shutting out the lies of Satan. Repentance and renewing our minds, therefore, is the only way to fight our fleshly natures and to ward off the onslaught of Satan and his demonic forces who seek at all costs to hold us in bondage. When we allow God to transform us, we change our appearance to look more like Jesus Christ. Behold the Man!

As our soul and body are renewed they become subject to our spirit. The soul and body (we sometimes call the "flesh") in right relationship with our spirit makes us one, (wholly sanctified). Paul's final prayer is that his converts might be wholly sanctified, that is, that their whole being spirit, soul, and body may *be fully yielded to the will of God"* (See 1 Thessalonians 5:23). I believe once we attain this level of sanctification our whole being becomes our heart, when we converse verbally or non-verbally our whole being is in agreement and glorifies God. The Holy Spirit working the Word in us brings us to this level; cleansing us from the inside out. Sanctification separates me from the world; however I am still Jay. The difference being my Christ-like character and behavior which is now God and others centered through love. The world no longer sees Adam, now they see Christ!

Deceitful Hearts

The Bible tells us that the heart is deceitful and unsearchable to any *but God* alone (see Jeremiah 17:9-10). Many of our churches are in disarray today; because we allow individuals who are not sanctified wholly to fill positions of leadership. The hearts of some people are so deceitful that they conceal who they really are until they are entrenched. It is imperative that we use discernment, much prayer and follow the Holy Spirit's guidance in these matters. As pastor, I have had to bite the bullet on several occasions when we did not follow the Spirit's guidance through the Word of God. One rotten apple can destroy the unity of the whole church. Certainly it is imperative that each candidate be saved, sanctified, and full of the Holy Spirit.

A deceitful heart causes many of us to deal with sin using only half-hearted measures, or to think that mental agreement to the Word of God is the same as obedience (See James 1:22). We need to ask God daily to search our hearts for sin that we cannot or will not see. This was David's prayer

(See Psalm 139:23-24). God's primary means of searching our hearts this way is through His Word, as we study, meditate, and pray under the power of the Holy Spirit. "The Word of God is living and sharper than any two-edged sword, dividing even the soul and spirit (See Hebrews 4:12). This means the Word is more effective than a surgeon's scalpel at cutting out that which is diseased. However, we must come to a place where we know that to be fact. When I was in basic military training, a primary duty of our platoon Sergeant early on was to instill in us just how important our rifles were to our survival. So important in fact that we had to eat and sleep with them. If we got careless and one of our leaders could sneak in and take it, we could look forward to some very harsh undesired disciplinary action. Needless to say, we not only learned to sleep with it but on it and though the lump was sometimes uncomfortable we got use to it.

The leadership spent numerous hours familiarizing us with the rifle, its manufacturer, its nomenclature, its capabilities under extreme conditions such as rain snow or freezing weather. We learned how to care for it so that it would continuously function properly in various extremes, even how to disassemble and assemble it blindfolded. All of this repetitious teaching and training paid off on the field of battle, unconsciously we made automatic responses to the changing environments, and we overcame the enemy's various deceptions and attacks.

Oh! What a difference if this kind of importance was put upon God's Word, in our training and preparation for discipleship and leadership in the local church. The Bible provides our daily spiritual nourishment for daily survival in all areas of our lives. As we were taught as soldiers, take care of your weapons and they will take care of you. So take care of the Word and it will take care of you.

Continual Cleansing through the Word (Bible)

A song I've heard the little tots sing in children's church goes something like this. Read your Bible and pray everyday, pray every day and you'll grow, grow, and grow. Don't read your Bible and pray everyday and you'll shirk, shirk, and shirk. There is so much truth in that little song. So many people encounter God's Word only through the weekly Sunday school, Bible study or the Sunday morning worship services. We must have a daily allotment of God's Word for the soul. Anemic Christians are not healthy Christians.

Additionally, many claim they can't find the time to read or study God's Word. They are totally oblivious of the fact that without the Word of God we can't possibly share the God life and promises that are our inheritance in this life on earth. We are raising a generation without the guidance of God's Word and certainly we see the results daily in the erosion of society's character and behavior. Relativism has become so ingrained in the American society. Having said all of that, let us not waver in the faith; and we know nothing is too hard for God.

True believers know the answer, the apostle of love, John admonishes *"But if we walk in the light as He is in the light, we have fellowship with one another, and the blood of Jesus Christ His Son cleanses us from all sin" (1 John 1:7).* The light is the love of God and the knowledge of God's Word. When we are driving at night, we can only see in the light our headlights provide; otherwise we are in darkness. Likewise, we can only see and walk according to the Word of God that we have; otherwise we will wander into darkness. It is our mission here at the Bread of Life Ministries to reach as many people as we possibly can with biblical doctrinal truth and training; that they might become spiritual beacons of light encouraging some and warning others. Inside and outside of the church of the dangers and erosion this distraction from the light of truth is causing the moral fibers of our families, churches, communities and this Nation to disintegrate.

Oh, to realize the importance of God's Word, and how it can transform your life. It is applicable to every circumstance and situation we experience in our life time. Notice what Jesus had to say about His Word, *"If you abide in Me, and My words abide in you, you will ask what you desire, and it shall be done for you" (John 15:7)*. Please notice, He did not say some of the things you desire, but what you desire. I said earlier, we should be the most healthiest and prosperous people on the planet. Why? God's Word promises it. Again, *"Beloved, I pray that you may prosper in all things and be in good health, just as your soul prospers" (2 John 3)*. Our *soul* comprised of our mind, will, and emotions all have tremendous bearing upon our individual as well as church health and prosperity. The Scriptures command that we be renewed in our minds; which means to change our thinking (world view).

We came into this world under the influence of parents, other family members, friends, peers, school, TV and the other media just to name a few that affects not only how we think but also what we think, and that's naturally so. However, once we are born again, our perspective must turn to the spiritual instead of the natural. In this perspective we see as God sees. We learn to agree with what He says about a matter. What He says to us through His Spirit and the Bible about any situation or circumstance of our life takes preeminence over anything we may ask or think. The apostle Paul admonishes that you not let this world (system) conform or shape you into its thinking (world view) but be transformed by the renewing of your mind, that you can personally know what God's will is for your life (see Romans 12:1-5).

This renewing of our minds is the work of the Holy Spirit and the Word of God. We can learn much from other people and other books, but what we learn in John 14 gives us great incite on God's perspective on the matter. The Bible has been called a roadmap to glory and that is certainly true, however, an upgrade to a GPS puts us right up to the door of any situation or circumstance, just plug in. God's word says, "Thy Word is a lamp unto my feet, and a light unto my path" (see Psalm 119:105).

How important is the Bible?

The apostle Peter admonishes us to "Grow in grace and the knowledge of our Lord and Savior, Jesus Christ." The Lord commanded Joshua, *"T his book of the Law shall not depart from your mouth, but you shall meditate in it day and night, that you may observe to do according to all that is written in it. For then you will make your way prosperous, and then you will have good success" (Joshua 1:8).*

This Book of the Law is a reference to the Scriptures, specifically Genesis through Deuteronomy, written by Moses (see Exodus 17:14; Deuteronomy 31:9-11, 24). Meditate on it means to linger over God's Word. I remember as a child watching cows eat grass and then in the heat of the day lying in the shade chewing their cud. At least that's what the old folks called it. In other words they would regurgitate what they had eaten earlier in the day and chew it up finer for digestion.

The lesson for us, here is that we must spend time in the Word and meditate or linger on it, chew on it, while applying by living it throughout the day. The Scripture is spiritual food, necessary for our total growth especially our thinking; thus they shall not depart from your lips. God charged Joshua with these words. Joshua at the time was being installed by God as the replacement for Moses. He now becomes the busiest man in the whole nation, yet God empresses upon him how imperative it is to meditate on His Word day and night. God promises to make his way prosperous and that he will have good success. (See Hebrews 5:14).

The principle here is central to all spiritual effort and enterprise, namely the deep understanding and application of the Scriptures *at all times.* It is essential that we develop a biblical world view. It is so sad, the number of Christians who attempt to apply a secular world view to their situations and circumstances even to those that are spiritual. It just doesn't make sense. Joshua helps us apply faithfully what we know about God's Word (See Joshua 1: 6, 7, 9; 15:63; 16:10; 17:12; others who used the Word of God for spiritual food are Job (Job 23:12); the Psalmist (Psalm 1:1-3); Jeremiah (Jeremiah 15:16); and Jesus, our Example (John 4:34). Behold the Man!

Now Alive to Christ

We are not only dead to sin, as we have seen thus far in this chapter; but we are alive to Christ. This comes as a result of "knowing" which does not mean to just know something about Christ nor understand some important doctrine. It is not an intellectual knowledge at all, but an opening of the eyes of your heart to see what we have in Christ.

How do you know your sins are forgiven? Is it because the pastor told you so? No, you just know it. If I ask you how you know, you'd simply answer, "I just know that I know." Such knowledge comes from revelation. It comes from the Lord Himself. Though the fact of forgiveness of sins is in the Bible, for the written Word of God to become a living Word from God to you He has to give you "a spirit of wisdom and revelation in the knowledge of Him" (See Ephesians 1:17). You need to know Christ in that way; it is the only way. So there comes a time, in regard to any new revelation of Christ, when you know it in your own heart, you "see" it in your spirit. The Holy Spirit has shined a light into your inner being and you are wholly persuaded of the fact.

What is true of the forgiveness of your sins (justification) is no less true of your deliverance from sin (sanctification). The apostle Paul assures us, *"And having been set free from sin, you become slaves of righteousness. I speak in human terms because of the weakness of your flesh. For just as you presented your members as slaves to uncleanness, and lawlessness leading to more lawlessness, so now present your members as slaves of righteousness for holiness" (Romans 6:18-19).* Here Paul uses the human analogy of slavery in appealing to holiness (consecration). In doing so he reminds us of the contrast between the old unregenerate life and the new regenerate life. Slaves of sin do not recognize the *obligation* to righteousness, but rather abandon themselves to a process of moral deterioration, which has death as its end, whereas, slaves of righteousness sanctify themselves to God, a road that leads to everlasting life.

If you ask a number of Christians who are experiencing the sanctified life of consecration how it came about some will say this way and others will say that way. Each stresses their own particular way of entering in and produces Scriptures to support their experience, it is so sad that Christians are using their experiences and their special Scriptures to fight other Christians. The fact of the matter is that, while Christians may enter into this life of consecration by different ways, we need not regard the experiences or doctrines they stress as mutually exclusive, but rather complementary. One thing is certain, that any true experience of value in the sight of God must have been reached by way of revelation of the Person and work of the Man, Jesus Christ. Behold the Man!

Personal Journal Notes

(Reflection & Response)

1. The most important thing that I learned from this chapter was:

2. The area that I need to work on the most is:

3. I can apply this lesson to my life by:

4. Closing Statement of Commitment

✣

Section 4
Victory In Jesus

CHAPTER 11

Sanctification: Has Standards

Biblical sanctification (holiness) like biblical justification is defined by the Lord in His Holy Word. Many think of sanctification as merely separating the sacred from the secular. For example, they separate themselves from certain people or other elements of society and only interface with other church folks. Often these people do not worship the Lord of glory nor have any true relationship with His Son, Jesus Christ our Lord and Savior. Sanctification not only means a separation from the world, but it also means a separation to God. While they are probably good, moral upstanding people in their community, in realty by God's standards of sanctification they are enemies of Christ because they actually serve the enemy.

The same can be said for many rituals and religious practices considered by some to meet the highest standards of separation, for instance dress, speech, foods, and even in some instances spiritual gifts. I knew a man personally who belonged to the same church that I belonged; who would not talk to others on his secular job, except as necessary to meet work requirements. He also brought his lunch and ate separately. To violate his standard would mean defilement and non-sanctity.

Personal preferences and standards are often presented in our churches as biblical doctrines when in reality they are not. Sometimes these commandments of men are taught with more passionate fervor than with the Scriptures. There is a natural tendency of men to allow the commandments of men and church traditions to become more important than God's commandments. God forbid!

The Bible teaches that those who teach that certain practices meet the biblical standards without true biblical backup are actually giving heed to deceiving spirits. Notice the warning words of Paul in 1Timothy 4:1-5:

"Now the Spirit expressly says that in latter times some will depart from the faith, giving heed to deceiving spirits and doctrines of demons, speaking lies in hypocrisy, having their conscience seared with a hot iron, forbidding to marry and commanding to abstain from foods which God created to be received with thanksgiving by those who believe and know the truth. For every creature of God is good, and nothing is to be refused if it is received with thanksgiving; for it is sanctified by the Word of God and prayer."

Some set standards for sanctification (holiness) which are established by men based on how they feel or think or what someone else has written outside of the Bible. These standards do not necessarily reflect biblical truth. Remember sanctification is defined by God, not men. If you have invented non-biblical practices that you deem right, you probably have opened yourself up to years of suffering, ungodly conduct and behavior. The apostle Paul further tells us,

"Therefore, if you died with Christ from the basic principles of the world, why, as though living in the world, do you subject yourselves to regulations? Do not touch, do not taste, do not handle; which all concern things which perish with the using according to the commandments and doctrines of men. These

things indeed have an appearance of wisdom in self-imposed religion, false humility, and neglect of the body, but are of no value against the indulgence of the flesh" (Colossians 2:20-23).

Sanctification is our witness to the outside world reflecting our Christ-likeness.

Personal Journal Notes

(Reflection & Response)

1. The most important thing that I learned from this chapter is:

2. The area that I need to work on the most is:

3. I can apply this lesson to my life by:

4. Closing Statement of Commitment

CHAPTER 12

Union: A New Creation

"*Therefore, if anyone is in Christ, he is a new creation; old things have passed away; behold, all things have become new" (II Corinthians 5:17).*

A New Creation

A new creation describes something that is created at a qualitatively *new level* of *excellence*. It refers to the Christian's forgiveness of sins paid for in Christ's substitutionary death, in regeneration, the new birth. The qualifying characteristic of this statement is to be *"in Christ."* These two words comprise a most profound statement of the Christian's redemption. We have been taught to think of ourselves as sinners needing redemption. For generations that has been instilled into us, and that is a great beginning, but it is not what God has in view for the end.

In Ephesians 5, we are told, Christ loved the church. There is something very precious here. God speaks rather of a glorious church, without spot or wrinkle or any such thing, but holy and without blemish. All too often we hear of the church as being merely so many saved sinners. It is that; but we have made the terms almost equal to one another, as though that was all there was to it; which is not the case. Saved sinners carry the thought of sin and the fall of man, but in God's sight the *church* is a divine new creation *in* His Son.

When you compare the two, the first is largely *individual,* the second *corporate.* The first view is negative and belonging to the past. These individuals seem to go through life viewing everything through the rearview mirror. However, the second view is positive, looking forward through the panoramic windshield. The *"eternal purpose"* is something in the mind of God from eternity concerning His Son, and it has as its objective that the Son should have a Body to express His life. Viewed from the standpoint of the heart of God, the Church is something which is *beyond* sin and *has never* been touched by sin.

The apostle John shares this view. He wrote, *"Whoever has been born of God does not sin, for His seed remains in him; and he cannot sin, because he has been born of God" (I John 3:9).*

I believe the seed that remains is the divine nature of which the Christian in Christ is a partaker (See 2 Peter 1:4). True Christians practice righteousness because the One in whom they dwell is righteous. God's righteousness is revealed in His children through their character and conduct. Righteous conduct does not produce righteous character, but reveals its presence in us. Therefore, those who are born of God do not sin because willful sin is not their nature. The Child of God's nature is righteousness as his or her Father is righteous; and the child of Satan's nature is to sin, like his or her father, the first sinner.

Truth and love are to be present and active in the life of every child of God. This requires a heart that is alert and can discern error and reject it. Study of the Word of God, prayer, meditation on the Word, and most importantly the Holy Spirit are the means by which Christians receives or rejects any doctrine. Guard your hearts and minds with great care.

In His farewell speech to His disciples, Jesus said, *"You are already clean because of the word which I have spoken to you" (John 15:3).* In this conversation He is anticipating the new creation and relationships which is to be obtained after His cross (see John 16:4). It is important to note that His first teaching concerning a Christian's present relationship to God concerns the cleansing of defilement, thus signifying its divine importance.

The way of salvation has been revealed in preceding chapters of John's Gospel; but beginning in John 13, He is speaking to those *who are saved,* and speaking to them of the divine cleansing from their defilement. He arose from supper, laid aside His outer garments, girded Himself with a towel (the insignia of a servant), poured water into a basin and began to wash the disciples' feet.

This is a miniature of a much larger undertaking, when He arose from the fellowship with His Father in heaven and laid aside the garments of His glory and humbled Himself, taking the form of a servant and became obedient unto death, even the death of the Cross, in order that we might be washed with the washing of regeneration (Titus 3:5).

In the larger undertaking there is the *whole* cleansing; but in the other there is a partial cleansing which is typified by the cleansing of the *feet only* of the one who is otherwise *completely clean (see John 13:10).*

This *two-fold cleansing* was also typified by the prescribed cleansing for the Old Testament priest. When he entered his ministry he was given a *ceremonial bath*, which was of his whole body, *once for all* (Exodus 29:4).

Yet he was required to *bathe his hands and his feet* at the brazen laver before *every* ministry and service in the Holy Place (See Exodus 30:17-21). So the New Testament Christian, though *once for all cleansed* as to his or her salvation, must also be cleansed from *every defilement,* and Christ alone can make him or her clean through the Spirit and the Word (See John 17). The brazen laver typifies Christ's cleansing through the Word of God and the Holy Spirit. (Review "the brazen laver" **"E" in Figure #1, on page 20).**

A person who willfully sins, even a believer is of the devil in the sense that he or she is participating in the devil's activity (See 2:19). The apostle John, the in-house expert witness in regard to the unbroken communion and fellowship with the Father and with His Son, writes these things that we also may have fellowship. God is light or He is perfect holiness. If we should say that we have fellowship with Him and are nevertheless walking in darkness, we lie and do not the truth (See 1 John 1:5). Walk in the truth of God's Word. To know truth requires acting on it.

On the other hand, if we walk in the light, as He is in the light, we have fellowship with the Father and with His Son, Jesus Christ. Please observe, sinless perfection is not demanded in this passage. It is not a command for the Christian to become the light, or what God alone is. However, He has required of us *confession,* when He convicts us of our sin, and that sin is to be dealt with *immediately.*

The passage goes on to point out the only recourse available in the Christian's life for sin: *"If we confess our sins, He is faithful and just to forgive us our sins, and to cleanse us from all unrighteousness" (1 John 1:9).* It is not mercy and kindness, He is faithful (to His child) and just to forgive (because of the atoning blood) *and it is all granted on the one condition of confession* (See 1 John 2:2; John 5:24).

Notice, we are nor forgiven of our sins because we ask to be forgiven. It is when we confess our sins that we are forgiven. Many are praying for forgiveness; but have made absolutely no confession of their sins. We understand further: *"For if we would judge ourselves, we should not be judged. But when we are judged, we are chastened of the Lord, that we should not be condemned with the world"* (See 1 Corinthians 11:31-32). The Father is here seen waiting for the *self* judgment or confession of His sinning child; but if the child will not judge himself or herself by a full confession of sin, then the Father *must* judge. If self-judgment is neglected, He must administer chastisement (See Hebrews 12:3-15). He cannot pass over the *unconfessed sin* of His child. The purpose in view here is *"That we should not be condemned with the world."* Chastisement is more than correction and punishment. The meaning of the word includes training and development. It therefore may be administered by the Father for the teaching and refining of the child. In 1 Corinthians 11:30, we see that chastisement may take many particular forms. Obedient Christians are abiding Christians.

For example in John 15:1-11 we are taught the importance of abiding in Christ:

- As we abide in Him, we are united to Him and His life flows through us and produces fruit.

- As the spiritual Christian abides in Christ he or she can bear lasting fruit.

- The fruitful branches are "purged" (v. 2, the same word as "clean" in v. 3) so they will bear more fruit. God cleanses us through His Spirit and the Word, chastening us to make us more fruitful, which helps to explain why a dedicated Christian often has to go through suffering.

- As believers abide they move from producing "fruit" to "more fruit" (v. 2) to "much fruit" (v. 8), they glorify the Father.

- The evidences of the abiding life are: the Savior's love (v. 9), obedience to His Word (v. 10), answered prayer (v. 7), and joy (v. 11), we get along with other believers; we love the brethren and get victory over the hatred of the world.

Listed in 1 Corinthians 11:30 are some of the results of not abiding in Christ:

- The branch that does not bear fruit is lifted out of its place of relationship to be with the Lord, compare this with the "many sleep" in 1 Corinthians 11:30.

- Failure to abide in Christ results also, in loss of effectiveness in prayer, loss of power in fruit-bearing and service, and can produce works instead of fruit.

- Loss of joy and fellowship in the Lord. The very weight of the hand of God can be exceedingly heavy. In II Corinthians 7:8-11, we see an example of true sorrow for the sin of a Christian. David is the outstanding example of true repentance and confession on the part of and Old Testament saint (see Psalm 51).

- For the Christian not to abide results in a backslidden state. This Christian is not lost as many interpret (v. 6), but need to repent and get back into the fight! We praise God that portions of the Old Testament passage that David prayed cannot rightly apply to a Christian in this dispensation of grace. We never have to pray, *"And take not thy Holy Spirit from me"(see Psalm 51) KJV;* for He came to abide forever (see Romans 5:5; Ephesians 4:30; John 6:27;

and 10:27-29). Again, to be a branch means to be united to Christ and share His life.

Concern yourself with God's Word becoming incarnate in you; and consider yourself as being under construction with Christ's likeness the objective.

A Present Help

But the anointing which you have received from Him abides in you, and you do not need that anyone teach you; but as the same anointing teaches you concerning all things, and is true, and is not a lie, and just as it has taught you, you will abide in Him (1 John 2:27).

The Anointing here refers either to the Holy Spirit or to the Scriptures. This anointing is the protection that believers have against false teachers. John says, these believers are different than the ones who went out (see John 2:19).

A Catastrophic Break

Please don't think that I would take one iota from the atonement and/ or redemption. Because we are still on the earth and the fall of man is a historic fact, redemption is imperative. The apostle Paul, speaking of Christ says, *"In Him we have redemption through His blood, the forgiveness of sins, according to the riches of His grace" (see Ephesians 1:7).*

But we must always view redemption as an interruption or catastrophic break in the straight line of God's purpose. The Fall is a tragic downward dip in the straight line of God's purpose and the atonement a blessed recovery whereby our sins are blotted out and we are restored; but when it is accomplished there remains a work to be done to bring us into possession of that which Adam never possessed, and to give God what His heart most desires. God has never forsaken His purpose which is represented by the straight line. Adam was never in possession of the life of God as presented in the tree of life.

Because of the one work of the Man, Jesus Christ our Lord, in His death and resurrection; His life was released to become *our life by faith.* As a result, we have received more than Adam ever possessed. Praise God! The very purpose of God is brought within reach of fulfillment in us by our receiving Christ as our life. Adam slept, and Eve was created out of him. That is God's method with the church. God's second Man has awakened from His sleep and His church was created in Him and of Him, to draw the life from Him and display that resurrection life to a dying world.

Many Brethren
God has a Son, His only begotten, and He seeks that the Son should have brethren. From the position of only begotten He will become the first begotten, instead of the Son alone. God will have many sons. One grain of wheat has died and as a result many grains will spring up. The first grain was once the only grain; now it has become the first of many. The Lord Jesus laid down His life, and that life emerged in many lives. In support of these biblical truths; Eve, the mother of all living, singular takes the place of the many. The outcome of the cross is shown to be one single person, a bride for the Son. Christ loved the church and gave Himself up for it.

In Romans 8, Paul speaks to us of Christ as the first-born Son among many Spirit-led sons of God (v. 14). The phrase as many as are led by the Spirit of God is more than a synonym for Christians. It describes the *lifestyle* of those who are *sons of God.* In this chapter Paul lays out two directions of life and shows their ultimate consequences. He implies that Christians have an ability to *choose* to do what is uncharacteristic of a Christian, namely, to walk "according to the flesh," and he warns not to do it. *If by the Spirit you put to death the deeds of the body:* A good summary of the process of sanctification (growth in holiness) in the Christian life.

We might summarize these chapters in Romans in this manner: Our sins are forgiven (Ch. 5), we are dead with Christ (Ch. 6), we are by nature utterly helpless (Ch. 7), *therefore* we rely upon the indwelling Spirit (Ch. 8). After this, and as a consequence of it: *So we being many are one body of Christ, and individually members, one of another (Romans 12:5).*

Paul calls for lives marked by humility and faithfulness in Christian relationships. Just as the physical body is made up of many members, each with a different function, the church is a body with many members, but all closely related and making up a unity *in Christ.* In Christ will be discussed fully in a later chapter.

Our different gifts and abilities should make us love and depend more on one another, and therefore we should by humility and faithfulness be more united as the one body of Christ. Note the new appeal to a higher level of consecration in Romans 6:13. Paul said, *"Present yourselves unto God, as alive from the dead, and your members as instruments of righteousness unto God."* But notice in Romans 12:1 the emphasis is a little different: *"I beseech you therefore, brethren, by the mercies of God, to present your bodies a living sacrifice, holy, acceptable to God, which is your reasonable service."* This new appeal for consecration is made to us as *"brethren,"* linking us to the *"many brethren"* of Romans 8:29. It is a call to us for a united *step of faith,* expressed in terms of the presenting of our bodies as *one* "living sacrifice" unto God.

One Living Sacrifice (Romans 12:1-5)

There is something that goes beyond the mere individual, for it implies a contribution to a whole. The presenting is personal *(the disciple),* but the sacrifice is corporate *(the church)*; it is *one* sacrifice. Intelligent service to God is one service. We should never feel that our contribution is not needed, for if it contributes to the service, God is satisfied. And it is through this kind of service that we prove *"what is the good and acceptable and perfect will of God (12:2)* or in other words, realize our part in God's eternal purpose in Christ Jesus. So Paul's appeal, to every man that is among you (12:3) is in the light of this new divine fact, that we who are many, are one body in Christ, and severally members one of another (12:5).

This is important. The vessel through which the Lord Jesus can reveal Himself in this generation is not the individual but the body. True, "God has dealt to each man a measure of faith" (12:3), but *alone in isolation* man can never fulfill God's purpose. It requires a complete body to attain to the stature of Christ and display His glory. Please Lord, that we should really understand this today, a day when individual (ism) strives to be king even in the local church. We tend to operate in a freedom that is not of God, and in many instances it's based on the opinions of men. God forbid.

Personal Journal Notes

(Reflection & Response)

1. The most important thing that I learned from this chapter was:

2. The area that I need to work on the most is:

3. I can apply this lesson to my life by:

4. Closing Statement of Commitment

CHAPTER 13

Ambassadors: Conformed to His Image

One important point for us to bring over from chapter 12 is the fact of many brethren and not Mr., Mrs., or Ms. Another point to keep in mind is the fact that transformation means changed to something else. Christ dwelt with our sins through His precious blood and He delivered us from the sin principle on Calvary. We are a new creation in Christ. Praise God! Therefore, Paul admonishes, those who live should live no longer for themselves; which is characteristic of the world; but we should now live for Christ who died and rose again. Therefore, anyone in Christ is a new creation. (See II Corinthians 5:15-17).

In Christ

In Christ is the most characteristic expression of what it means to be a Christian. Christ's death and resurrection for us, and our identification with Him in that death and resurrection by faith, makes our existence as a new creation possible.

Old things, legalism, secular thinking and ungodly worldview, negative strongholds, unethical behavior are all passed away, because our minds have been renewed through the truths of God's Word. Folks, I cannot stress enough how much our very life depends on our developing the disciplines of a personal daily time of devotions consisting of prayer, Bible study, and meditation of the Word. We must let the glory of God shine through us as we live out that Word in all areas of life daily.

We are now incorporated into God's eternal plan of many sons. Thus, we no longer think only as an individual, but now as a part of the corporate body of Christ. Now that we are in Christ, His purpose becomes our purpose.

The Ministry of Reconciliation

The Scripture says, *Now all things are of God, who has reconciled us to Himself through Jesus Christ, and has given us the ministry of reconciliation, that is, that God was in Christ reconciling the world to Himself, not imputing their trespasses to them, and has committed to us the word of reconciliation (2 Corinthians 5:18-19).*

Those of us who are already reconciled have been given the ministry of reconciliation. That is, we have been commissioned to bring the message and witness to others. The message of what God, who was in Christ, has done to provide atonement for sin. The Gospel or Good News is the ministry of all believers, what I call our personal pulpits. This message of reconciliation has all but disappeared in many local churches and also in the public square today. Remember, the Gospel is the message the Bible says, is the power of God unto salvation.

Ambassadors for Christ

In 1959 as a soldier in the U. S. Army, I was assigned Mannheim, Germany. Once there, all new arrivals had to undergo a period of training concerning our conduct as U. S. soldiers assigned to a foreign country. After many hours of orientation we came to see ourselves as ambassadors. We were told that we were representatives of the government of the United States. As a result everything we did and everywhere we went reflected on the United

States of America. A better example of an ambassador came many years later when I was assigned in 1980 – 1982, to duty in Seoul, Republic of South Korea.

My family accompanied me on this assignment. The nature of the assignment enabled us to live in diplomatic Embassy housing. On occasions, I had to attend Command and Staff meetings which included the American Ambassador to South Korea. As ambassador, he was the direct representative of the president and the government of the United States. Everything he conveyed was from President Reagan. He had no personal messages or opinions about anything. He served at the pleasure of the president.

The housing area in which we lived was self-contained, actually a little part of America, a colony or island in a foreign land. Accordingly, we did not have to rely on the host country for anything. We had our own church, hospital, schools, shopping areas, recreational facilities and areas for sports, golf, hunting, fishing or whatever. In other words all of our needs had to be met by our homeland, America. Our Commander in Chief was responsible for all of our needs to include our safety. We were in Korea but not of Korea. We were Americans in a foreign land. It was expected of us to live the part in our behavior and conduct. It was a very rewarding assignment and very enjoyable; but we all looked forward to going home one day; and receiving our medals and awards from a grateful nation.

Paul gives us this same kind of orientation. We are in the world but our citizenship is in heaven. We are ambassadors for Christ, the King of heaven. Our task is to convey His message to the people of the world to be reconciled to God who is their rightful King (see Romans 10:13-18). We are responsible to Him for the accuracy of how we communicate that message. He has given us explicit instructions in the Holy Bible concerning the conduct of all areas of our lives. We walk by faith not by sight. He has promised to supply our every need and also to never abandon us. He is faithful. We enjoy our assignment here, but look forward to going home one day; where we look forward to a "well done" from our King.

Walk in the Spirit

To be the Lord's ambassadors or ministers of reconciliation requires that we be positive in character, conformed to the image of the Son of God. The Christian has no power within himself or herself to accomplish this. The Scriptures assure us that we can attain this by reliance upon the presence and power of the indwelling Holy Spirit. *"This I say then, by means of the Spirit be walking, and you shall not fulfill the lust of the flesh" (Galatians 5:16).*

Rightly divided, the Scriptures do not make the impossible demand upon the Christian that he or she in their human strength is to accomplish a *"walk in the Spirit."* The Scriptures reveal that the Spirit will do the walking in the Christian. Therefore, the human responsibility is total dependence upon the Spirit.

The life that God honors is always the divine objective in the Christian's daily life. It's never realized by human resolution, struggle or the resources of the flesh, but only by *fighting the good fight of faith.* There is a vast difference between fighting to do what God alone can do, and fighting to *maintain an attitude of dependence on Him* for what He alone can do. The child of God has the responsibility of continuing in an attitude of reliance upon the Spirit. This is his or her constant attention. This is the divinely appointed task and place of cooperation in the mighty purpose of God. Only then can the Spirit possess and renew every human faculty, emotion, and choice.

Three Hindrances to the Indwelling Spirit

The Bible assigns at least three hindrances to the Christian's constant reliance upon the indwelling Spirit:

- *The contrast of the impossible heavenly standard of life versus the world standard.*

God has but one Book and that Book includes all people of every dispensation. In it we find His will and purpose. The Bible also contains a rule of life which applies to the Christians of this present day; who though heavenly in position and responsibility, are called upon to live as "pilgrims and strangers" in the earth and as witnesses in enemy territory.

These governing principles are found in the Book of Acts, the epistles and portions of the Gospels. These heavenly standards are not imposed on the unregenerate world; since they have not received the Holy Spirit. It is both useless and unreasonable to apply Christian standards to an unregenerate world. In the Scriptures, Christians are addressed as, a supernatural people with a superhuman manner of life placed upon them. Certainly this is reasonable.

Christians are citizens of heaven from the moment they are saved and it is naturally required of them that they *walk worthy of their heavenly calling.* They are not made citizens of heaven by any earthy means; but by the power of God. It becomes Christians to live according to the position that God has given them. The following passages will illustrate the superhuman character required of the Christian under grace.

"A new commandment I give you, that you love one another; as I have loved you" (John 13:34). The Law required love to be to another *"as yourself."* To love as Christ has loved us is infinitely higher, and humanly *impossible.*

"Bringing into captivity every thought to the obedience of Christ" (II Corinthians 10:5). Though these passages present impossible demands upon the human resource, God expects them to be lived out in every Christian's daily life. The Holy Spirit indwells the Christian for this very purpose.

- *The Christian faces Satan.*

The Bible presents Satan as the enemy of the saints of God and especially is this true of the saints of this age. There is no controversy between Satan and unsaved people; for they are a part of his world system. They have not been delivered from the powers of darkness and translated into the kingdom of the Son of God. Satan is the energizing power in those who are unsaved (see Ephesians 2:2), as God is the energizing power in those who are saved (see Philippians 2:13). Every human being is either under the power of Satan, or under the power of God. We are not implying that Christians may not be influenced by Satan or that the unsaved may not be influenced by the Spirit of God; but their allegiance is in one domain or the other, and Satan's domain is not in all matters characterized by things that are inherently evil; as those things are estimated by the world.

Satan's life-purpose is to be "like the Most High" (see Isaiah 14:14), and he appears "as an angel of light," and his ministers, "as the ministers of righteousness" (see II Corinthians 11:13-15). His false ministers of *righteousness* preach a positive gospel of reformation and salvation by *human character*, rather than salvation by *grace alone through faith* unrelated to human efforts. Therefore, the world with all of its moral standards and culture is not necessarily free from the power and energizing control of Satan.

As we can see virtually across America today Satan will promote forms of religion and human excellence *apart from the redemption that is in Christ,* and the world is evidently more conditioned each day to undertake that very deception. He has blinded the unsaved concerning one thing only; they are blinded by Satan lest the light of the gospel should shine unto them (see II Corinthians 4:3, 4).

The thrusts of Satan's "fiery darts" are aimed at God who dwells within us. However, the conflict is real and the enemy is supernatural. The Scriptures commands: *"Finally my brethren, be strong in the Lord, and in the power of His might. Put on the whole armor of God that you may be able to stand against the wiles of the devil. For we wrestle not against flesh and blood, but against the rulers of the darkness of this age, against spiritual hosts of wickedness in heavenly places" (Ephesians 6:10-12).*

The Bible does not sanction the foolish belief promoted by some that Satan will flee at the mere resistance of a determined human will. We are to *"resist the devil,"* but it must be done steadfast in the faith, and while we are submitting ourselves to God (See James 4:7; I Peter 5:9). A Christian with his or her limitations must appeal to the power of God in the conflict with this mighty enemy, and he or she is directed to do this: *"Above all, taking the shield of faith, with which you shall be able to quench the fiery darts of the wicked one" (Ephesians 6:16).* The Christian's conflict with Satan is as fierce and unceasing as this mighty being can make it. Before him we of ourselves are as nothing; but God has anticipated our helplessness and provided a perfect victory through the indwelling Holy Spirit. Remember: *"Greater is He that is in you, than he that is in the world" (1 John 4:4).*

- *Careless Christians who are not concerned with the Person and work of the Holy Spirit.*

Satan has pitfalls and counterfeit doctrines all over the landscape; false teachings about sin especially the sin question as related to the Christian.

Daily, we hear many sermons with a "does better" theology, and little or no "trust God" truths. It seems the gospel of Christ is reserved for Easter. As a result, we are raising a generation of young people with little or no appreciation for God or His Holy Word.

Therefore their help from the Scriptural provisions such as knowing that the Word of God is *"profitable for doctrine, for reproof, for correction, for instruction in righteousness: that the man of God may be perfect, thoroughly furnished unto all good works" (II Timothy3:16, 17);* and in the same epistle to "study" and "rightly divide" the Word of truth are unknown to them.

Please note, two out of four of the values of the Scriptures in the life of the "man or woman of God," as recorded in the above passage are *"reproof"* and *"correction";* yet how few, especially of those who are holding an error have a teachable spirit. Seemingly, one of the characteristics of all satanic error is that those who have embraced it seem to never desire reconsidering their stand. They read only, misleading material that supports the error and avoid any opportunity to hear corrective teaching from the Word of God.

Sadly, those in error have made tremendous inroads into areas where our young people are the most vulnerable, our colleges, universities and the media. Those institutions seem to be getting there first with the most. While watching religious programming on TV, it occurred to me that the majority of those listening and watching are probably established Christians. How much of the Good News is heard in the secular arena of the media? As a pastor, I have tried to counsel the teens in the pastorate sometimes through sermons, one on one, and even in small groups to help ease the coming culture shock they will face when they move out for college, the military or just on their own. Many of them are returning home disillusioned and in total despair; because they were unprepared for the great deception called the world.

I was watching the news a few days ago and I was hit with culture shock. One of our leading universities announced plans to allow the students to select their own roommates and gender is not a consideration. Relativism (truth is relative and determined by the individual) is really making inroads in this country; in many cases, leaving parents and churches behind. In my book *How Should We Then Live,* I expound on some of the words that our society has redefined. For example, traditional tolerance defined in Webster's dictionary means to recognize and respect the beliefs, and practices of others, without sharing them. Additionally, to bear or put up with someone or something not especially liked. However, the new definition says that every individual's beliefs, values, lifestyles, and perceptions are equal. So our politicians pass laws and make rules in the name of choice, privacy, and free speech, knowing that they will cause character and morals to fly right out the window. What we've done is create another world system. The prince of this world, Satan and his demonic powers are behind these systems. System is defined as a method or way of doing something; which has an affect on the whole. These world systems are the children of academia, corporation board rooms, the media, and social scientists just to name a few. Since they are temporal, we know that they do not have the power to go as far as needed in fixing the problems. Therefore, containment is considered the norm.

The world is defined as the planet Earth; the universe; the human race; or a field of human interest or effort. This fourth definition applies here. So putting these two words together gives us great insight into what is happening within our Nation. We hear it used everyday: the world of sports, the world of finances, the world of economics, the world golf, the world of justice, and even the world of religion. We have no idea how these various worlds operate until we have to interact with them. Then we find that they play by their own set of rules; even establishing their own ethics. So the university situation I mentioned above is from the world of higher education, academia.

Much of what is heard as news whether it be from religious or secular stations is from the world of broadcasting. America has so many religions today competing for the souls of men. What is frightening is the fact that more and more we see a hybrid of the local church coming to power inclusive of these various religions. Their actions are also hidden under what the post moderns call multicultural (ism). This insensitivity shows that more and more Christians are not relying on the Holy Spirit for guidance. Therefore, little if anything they are about concerns Jesus Christ and God's plan for the redemption of man. One of the major reasons for this hatred and rejection of Christianity is the fact that; Christianity is exclusive and not inclusive (see John 3:3). Certain Bible truths and standards must be met before the individual can be accepted.

As a part of the new creation, each saved person has the responsibility to take the truth of God's Word to the world. While theologians continue to argue about genders in the pulpit and doubt the priesthood of all believers; it is imperative that those of us in present truth get about our Father's business. In our priestly roles we are to take our personal pulpit (spiritual not physical) and minister wherever the need is presented. Living out our knowledge of Christ invites others to want what we have in Christ. The Word of God alone without the life is not effective. In fact, it is probably more damaging. Christ like character with the Word of God in action is the only way.

Personal Journal Notes

(Reflection & Response)

1. The most important thing that I learned from this lesson was:

2. The area that I need to work on the most is:

3. I can apply this lesson to my life by:

4. Closing Statement of Commitment

CHAPTER 14

Saints: The Highest Calling

The greatest calling on earth is to be a saint of the Most High God. There is no higher privilege or position than that of being a child of God through the Man, Jesus Christ our Lord and Savior. The apostle Paul wrote to the saints at Ephesus that he was praying for them:

That the God of our Lord Jesus Christ, the Father of glory, may give to you the spirit of wisdom and revelation in the knowledge of Him, the eyes of your understanding being enlightened; that you may know what is the hope of His calling, what are the riches of the glory of His inheritance in the saints, and what is the exceeding greatness of His power toward us that believe, according to the mighty working of His mighty power (Ephesians 2:17-19).

As we saw in the last chapter, the saints of God are those who have been given the privileged opportunity to be conformed to the image of Jesus Christ. This means not only the conforming of our inward character, attitudes, and desires, but also becoming like Jesus, our Example, in all our character, behavior and interactions with those around us. I do believe that we are in a period of restoration of the saints to their rightful place of empowerment by the Holy Spirit. As a result, the average saint will demonstrate the supernatural works of Jesus Christ not only in the church environment, but also in the marketplace unashamedly.

The Corporate Body of Saints – The Church

At the end of Luke's record (see Acts 27 for full account), of the church's early history, he, Paul, and a few other saints arrived in Rome. Paul was held under house arrest. It was the minimum form of security, and that worked well for Paul. He asked for a meeting with the Jewish saints first and spent his days sharing his faith the Scriptures say, *from morning till evening" (Acts 28:23). For two whole years Paul stayed there in his own rented house and welcomed all who came to see him (v. 30).*

"Boldly and without hindrance he preached the kingdom of God and taught about the Lord Jesus Christ" (v. 31). While those are the finishing words for the Book of Acts, the Book has no ending. For some reason the next page was never written. Or perhaps the pages are still being written, today.

As we look back at the beginning of the book, we find these words: *Looking back to the beginning of the book, Luke wrote: The former account I made, O Theophilus of all that Jesus began both to do and to teach, until the day in which He was taken up, after He through the Holy Spirit had given commandments to the apostles whom He had chosen (Acts 1:1-2).* These verses reveal the transfer of Christ's work, authority, and mission to His disciples.

After Jesus ascended back to heaven, He divided His ministry mantle into five different kingdom tasks that He gave as gifts to certain members of His Body, the Church. He gave specific names which by all rights are self-descriptive job descriptions to these gifted ministers. The Scripture says, *"And He Himself gave some apostles, some prophets, some evangelists, some pastors, and some teachers" (see Ephesians 4:11).* Several terms or phrases have been employed to describe these five gifts given to both men and women of God:

- The ascension gifts of Christ

- Fivefold minister and fivefold ministry

- The governmental and administrative offices of the Church

Technically speaking, these are not gifts of the Holy Spirit but gifts of Christ Himself to the body of Christ. I have been a five-fold ministry teacher for the past 42 years. It has been a joyous experience as our Lord has allowed me to operate across denominational lines freely; so I am a body minister. Much of the resistance I have faced over the years has been from the denomination that I was raised up in. The Holy Spirit and the spiritual gifts that He give to members of the local church are essential if the church is to have life and operate decently and in order. When the Holy Spirit is recognized as the giver of gifts the works of the flesh will be bound. While there is no particular Scripture that states what particular things evangelists, pastors, and teachers do. There are specific Scriptures that state what apostles and prophets do. In Ephesians 2:20, we see that the apostles and prophets are foundational ministers upon which the rest of the members of the body are built. They provide the structure for the equipping and activation of the saints into their spiritual gifts and ministries.

Day of the Saints

The last sentence of the Book of Acts says of Paul, *"Boldly and without hindrance he preached the kingdom of God and taught about the Lord Jesus Christ" (v. 31).* So how did Paul live? *Boldly!* He may not have had a tomorrow, but he had today. Knowing that death may soon come, as he waited on a court date; he welcomed visitors and preached to those who would listen.

What happened? God's power kept working. I wonder what Paul would think of his influence today? The letters he wrote to churches from Corinth to Philippi, to the believers right there in Rome, to new preachers like Timothy and Titus, and changed men like Philemon, and wrote more than half of the New Testament. So Paul's influence isn't confined to the first century churches. God continues to use Paul two thousand years later through his writings *billions* of people have been affected for the kingdom.

Aren't you glad that Paul didn't chicken out under the threat of death in Rome; just give up and quite? Surely that would have been the natural thing to do, but Paul was not natural and neither are we. The passage quoted on the last page of Acts is from Isaiah, one of the boldest prophets of the Old Testament. The Book of Isaiah contains sixty-six chapters and more than thirty-five thousand words. The few words that Paul quoted therefore, are obviously important, he did not chose them by accident. Being filled with the Holy Spirit, I'm sure the Spirit brought them to his remembrance.

The words came from Isaiah's most *personal* encounter with God, an encounter that filled Isaiah with the *power of his purpose.* Isaiah's powerful encounter was recorded in Isaiah 6:1-7. There he saw smoke, heard the sounds, and saw the brilliance of God in his glimpse of heaven. Seraphim (an order of angels) hovered over the Lord and sang, "Holy, holy, holy is the Lord Almighty; and the whole earth is full of His glory" (v.3).

Isaiah fell on his face and screamed, "Woe is me!" (v.5). When Isaiah thought he was a goner from being in the presence of God, he was saved by an unusual event. In a moment, a seraph brought a coal from the altar and touched Isaiah's lips. The red-hot coal seared away the sin and made a sinful man clean, *ready* for a conversation with God.

Then I heard the voice of the Lord saying, "Whom shall I send? And who will go for us? And I said, "Here am I, Send me!" He said, "Go tell this people: "Be ever hearing, but never understanding; be ever seeing, but never perceiving; Make the heart of this people calloused; make their ears dull and close their eyes. Otherwise they might see with their eyes, hear with their ears, understand with their hearts, and turn and be healed" (Isaiah 6:8-10).

According to the last sentences of Acts, it's these words, from this story, that Paul focused on in the last season of his preaching. Filled with the Holy Spirit, power, knowledge, and experience, this mature saint went back to the basics with his final words.

He returned to his own powerful personal encounter with God quoting instructions from Isaiah's encounter, as he invites listeners in Rome to have their own powerful encounter.

Like Isaiah, Paul had received forgiveness first and mission second. Both became men greatly anointed of God, but nothing could happen until both had experienced a personal encounter with the Lord. The power of knowing their purpose came after both men knew the power of confession and forgiveness.

Today, nothing has changed. You can have the same anointing described in Acts but not before you've had that personal encounter. Paul couldn't move forward without forgiveness. You can't, I can't and neither could Isaiah.

Once Isaiah had an encounter with the living God, he went on a mission so empowered by the Holy Spirit, the world never forgot him. Once Paul had an encounter with the Lord, he was ready to deliver a new message, the completed story of how God had given the ultimate blood sacrifice through His Son, the Man, Jesus Christ. Both of these men experienced supernatural power, that was beyond belief; but it was also real.

It is imperative that the saints experience the same encounter wherein we meet the Lord personally today. If you have not had this encounter, but desire it:

- Repent, admit you are a sinner. *The Bible says we've all sinned and fallen short of God's glory (Romans 3:23).*

- Believe in your heart, the Lord Jesus, that He is the Son of God (John 3:16).

- Confess with your mouth, the Lord Jesus as your personal Savior and the Bible promises that you are saved (see Romans 10:9-13). So now that you've been restored, redeemed, and cleansed; consecrate your life to living, and to use Luke's last words in Acts, "boldly and without hindrance" (28:31). The next page of Acts could be up to you, so get to it.

Equipped for Service

The five ministers of Ephesians 4:11; that we discussed earlier in this chapter have been assigned by Christ to equip the saints so that the *saints* will be able to:

- Do the work of ministry and

• The *saints* will be able to edify or build up the body of Christ (see 4:12).

The Greek word *katartismos* (Eph. 4:12) is variously translated as "equip," or "perfect." An examination of how *katartismos* and its related family of words as used in the Scriptures will help us grasp the scope of equipping ministry and the environment which must be cultivated for ministry in the local church.

Selected New Testament Passages

Some examples for "equip" are as follows: When Jesus called James and John to be disciples, they are *mending* their nets (see Matthew 4:21; Mark 1:19). A disciple will be fully taught when he is like his teacher (See Luke 6:40). Addressing the division in the church at Corinth, Paul urges the congregation to *"be united* in the same mind" (1 Corinthians 1:10). He prays for the *improvement* of the Corinthians and exhorts them to *mend* their ways (2 Corinthians 13:9, 11). Christians are to intervene in the lives of those who have stumbled by *restoring* them in a spirit of gentleness (Galatians 6:1). Paul hopes to come to the Thessalonians to *supply* what is lacking in their faith (1 Thessalonians 3:10). Of Christ's incarnation, Hebrews 10:5 states, "A body was *prepared* for Him." By the Word of God the world was *created* (Hebrew 11:3). Christ is sufficient to *equip* us for every good work (Hebrews 11:21) and to *establish* us in our faith after a trail (1 Peter 5:10).

From these Scriptures, we glean three Equipping Ministries:

I. The Equipping Ministry of Restoration (see Matthew 4:21; 9:27; Mark 1:19; 1 Corinthians 1:10:13:9, 11; Galatians 6:1; 1 Thessalonians 3:10). Restoring includes:

- Bringing the disciple back to the *original* state of *wholeness* in Christ.

When the Holy Spirit begins this process of restoration, He has placed us into a new season of life and ministry. While God's principles and truths never change His methodology does change. These new methods are presented to the body of Christ, the church, as "new wine." I think that some people confuse the new wine with new wineskins. The first thought of many is to get rid of the old wineskin. Certainly that is true when we consider the Scriptures. However this is the Holy Spirit's operation. Most of us are familiar with Matthew 9:27 that says, *"Nor do they put new wine in old wineskins, or else the wineskins break, the wine is spilled, and the wineskins are ruined. But they put new wine into new wineskins, and both are preserved."*

The Holy Spirit is taking the true church of God through a period of restoration. Placing saints back to their rightful place of a kingdom of priests doing the work of ministry. As I stated earlier, not a kingdom of passive people led by a priest. In order to contain the new wine of restoration, we need a new wineskin. The Greek word for new is *"neos."* But that is not the word used in this passage. The word used here is *"kainos,"* meaning something that has been renewed or made over, something new.

To make a wineskin new, He soaks the old wineskin water (the Word of God) and rubs in the oil (the Holy Spirit); but that oil also contains a new anointing. In this restorative process, God takes what was there and brings it to a new place so that He can pour within it that which He longs to release, new wine to His people. As we allow the Holy Spirit to take us through the process of rubbing we not only become more pliable and flexible, but we can handle all that God desires to pour into us, and we are able to pour out in greater measure.

For the past twelve years my wife and I have been operating as new wineskins. We founded the Bread of Life Bible Institute for the sole purpose of pouring out the new wine of restoration to the people of God. I was privileged to pastor four traditional churches during the past 28 years. During that entire period I was pegged as a radical mainly because I believed in and practiced a Spirit-filled, Spirit-led life and ministry and strived to lead the church to do the same. When I say this, I most certainly include my wife of 48 years, Magdalene, who went through the washing and rubbing with me. In each church I taught a walk of faith through the Holy Spirit and the Word of God. Insuring that, each disciple recognizes the fact that the gifts of the Spirit are activated by love. I strived to live and encouraged the people to live out the lessons taught. There were victories, losses and casualties.

There exists a core group of saints whom the Lord raised up to walk with my wife and me in ministry. Some have been with us for the entire 28 years others came on board through the years. Jesus said when a disciple is mature he or she is like their teacher (my paraphrase). I assure you that statement is true. Since we founded the Bread of Life Ministries International, which comprise a non-traditional Bible Institute and a Church planting ministry. We have planted nine churches in North Carolina and other States and established ten satellite Bible Institute campuses, five in North Carolina (Headquarters) and five in other States. About 90% of the leadership of both the churches and schools are the products of the Bread of Life's disciple-making mission (teaching them).

We are new wineskins (old restored wineskins) pouring out the new wine of restoration, restoration of biblical doctrinal truth that once guided the church (see Jude 3). Our mission is pouring the new wine into the saints producing mature disciples who go forth with a biblical worldview, and in turn pouring out to others who do the same (see 2 Timothy 2:2).

So how does the wineskin change? First of all a removal must occur. We must take the limits off God. The Scripture says, nothing is too hard for God. Either we believe that or we really don't trust God's Word. I am seventy years old taking absolutely no medication not even an aspirin regimen. My annual physicals are without incident. During my 28 years of pastoral ministry I have never missed a Sunday service or Wednesday night meeting because of sickness. I teach divine healing to folk around the world in the classroom, on audio and video, how can I teach truth if I don't walk in it myself?

I was led of the Holy Spirit to step down from the pastorate six months ago to pour out through teaching and writing. My first book *"How Should We Then Live?"* was published about a month later in July 2010 and is available on line or anywhere Christian books are sold. This is my second book and it is scheduled for release in the spring of this year. The Spirit has moved my wife and me into a new place to pour out the new wine. Notice, at a time when most 70 year olds are beginning to draw in, the Lord is launching us into a full time International ministry. To God goes the glory!

A great example of how I view the new wineskin can be seen in John the Baptist and Jesus. Many are teaching that Jesus is the new Wineskin and John the Baptist is the old wineskin. Please note John the Baptist was the last of the old wineskin prophets. However, he was different in the fact that the Holy Spirit did not come upon him, but in him in his mother's womb. So though he was the old wineskin the Holy Spirit took him and not just him, but the office of the prophet through the process of restoration. Why was his nemesis the prophet Elijah? Actually I see John the Baptist, the new wineskin, and Jesus Christ is the new wine poured out.

Many of us remember the days of the old carbon copy paper. After a number of uses it would lose its effectiveness and much of the message could not be understood, even blurred, and in some cases part of the text was completely missing. The way to clear up the problem was to go back to the original copy. John the Baptist full of the Holy Spirit poured out and into us Christ, the new Wine. The New Wine becomes our very life, John baptized with water, but this New Wine Christ baptizes with fire and the Holy Ghost *[denotes two actions].*

As a well-traveled pastor and Bible teacher I find myself totally disappointed with many of the local churches I visit *(the fire is waning or gone out).* Perhaps we should review the tabernacle of Exodus. *The fire that consumed the sacrifice on the brazen altar came down from heaven and for 1500 years that original fire had to be kept burning.* All sacrifices on the brazen altar had to be lit from that *original fire sent from heaven.* That was the service of an order of priests (keep the fire burning!). We read of some priests who tried to duplicate the fire with their own "strange fire." That only led to their demise.

An important lesson to be learned here is the fact that old wineskins are God's wineskins as well as the new wineskins. In fact we see from the above example, at one time the old wineskin was God's new wineskin. The priests had to watch and keep their physical eyes on that natural flame for 1500 years to insure that it did not go out.

There are a lot of priests in the churches to day with "strange fire" claiming that their fire is the new wine. God for bid! Christ, the New Wine has been poured out once, that's it folks! Once for all! He brought the fire and the Holy Ghost to His body, the church. After 2000 years of duplication the message is getting garbled and in some cases completely blurred or missing.

There is a place for us old wineskins in God's plan today. That place is to allow the Holy Spirit to restore us to the original (new wineskin), so that we can properly carry the new wine to this generation. We must keep the truth of God's Word burning in our own hearts and the hearts of men. 2000 years ago Jude called it the faith *once* delivered to the saints.

The essence of the priesthood of all believers is the fact that all of us have the responsibility of keeping the Fire (Christ) alive in our hearts and passing Him on to our children and our children's children. During my 26 ½ years in the U.S. Army, I traveled all over the world and that includes the jungles of South America, the jungles of Vietnam, Islands in the Pacific and the Atlantic. In the remotest places some with almost no sign of civilization as we know it. One thing that stood out was Coca Cola had already been there. The Coca Cola signs were there; some marking the village store or as a patch on a hut, but coke was present. After seeing these signs everywhere, I'm sure some people would be curious to know why the company spends so much money on advertisement. Gracious they are already everywhere! Their explanation and ours should be similar.

Every day millions die who knew of Coca Cola and everyday there are millions born who have never heard of Coca Cola. The company must keep up an aggressive advertisement campaign. Every day millions die who heard of Jesus; but everyday millions are born who've never heard of Christ. We have got to keep up an aggressive campaign on His behalf. It has been said, we are one generation away from Christianity's extinction. If one generation drops the ball the next generation won't hear about Christ.

No, No those of us who know Him will not retire; if we let Him, Christ will continue to restore us to another place of service right on up until we draw our last breath on this side. Many of us have ministered to many people over the years; now as old restored wineskins we can now pass on the fire to those who have never known Christ as we have! There's a lot of good ground out there, get to your task of planting.

Opportunities for ministry are everywhere. Remember if there was not a Barnabas there would have not been an apostle Paul? Barnabas means son of encouragement. How the people need this ministry today. Rest homes, hospitals, the check out clerks, the college professor, the student, the government official, I could go on and on. The bottom line is the harvest is still great, but the laborers are so few.

• Dealing with the priests of strange fire.

Many of the worship services have turned into just another variety show "strange fire." Some of the praise dancers, choirs and even some pastors are entertaining the folks and making them feel good. Satan is pleased! Some well-intentioned pastors are bringing in the "strange fire" of non Christian rock and rap groups supposedly to attract youth. Whatever we are doing *it* must be *"as unto the Lord."* Just this week, I read a recent Barna survey that his group took of several thousand teens. The results of a question about what they wanted most from their church: Would you believe the majority wanted to be taught Bible doctrine. In other words, they wanted truth. Not the trips, not the concerts and socials, but the truth.

Another "strange fire" observation, many of the local churches are allowing unsaved people to join the assembly and participate fully in the life of the church; and as a result the Spirituality of the church suffers and foundational truths are lost or ignored as the church eventually slips into compromise. Many are parading in new theologies, at the expense of the apostles' doctrinal teaching and training as found especially in the Book of Acts, and other New Testament Books. The restoration of biblical truth in the local church is a most needful restoration ministry. *Spiritual and Biblical ignorance is Satan's secret weapon against the local church.* We must begin to:

- Restore the people to proper *alignment* after he or she has done something to put them out of alignment with Christ.

Therefore a restoration ministry exercises discipline. The church as a therapeutic community accepts people as they are, but loves them enough not to allow them to remain that way. Paul admonishes that those who are spiritual should *restore* such a one (see Galatians 6:1). This may require intervention by a spiritual leader who shares insight with the pastor, or a small group ministry.

- Restoring to *supply* what is *lacking.*

Circumstances of life shift around us, many people allow these circumstances to shape their view of the Word of God. Rather than allowing the Word of God to shape their view of their circumstances. The results are fear and wrong choices in many cases. This requires the building up of faith through the Word of God and a ministry of encouragement. Ministries associated with pastoral care such as hospital visitation, bereavement, counseling, and crisis intervention, all focused on supplying what is lacking. The ministries associated with restoration have traditionally been the work of ordained ministers. Churches have hired pastors to take care of them as if this ministry was an end in itself; the pastor has been to the church what a doctor is to a hospital. From a pastoral point of view, I see this as a major obstacle in the ministry of restoring the church to a ministry of all believers. Even with professional training many pastors of failing traditional churches refuse to see that equipped saints doing the ministry is the biblical focus. Ministry preparation must be on wholeness so that the people of God can become effective ministers. People are put back together again so that they can be useful channels in the service of the Lord. Failure to build up the body of Christ with whole people cripples our opportunities of bringing the message of salvation and the witness of God's glory to a broken and lost world.

II. The Ministry of Establishing and Laying Solid Foundations (see Luke 6:40;

Hebrews 11:5; 13:21; 1 Peter 5:10).

There are three aspects of establishing and laying solid foundations:

- Jesus Christ, the true Foundation,

- The Word of God, and

- Example, the Incarnation Way:

Jesus is the true Foundation
When it comes to laying foundations, Jesus Christ is described as the Head Equipper. Notice this passage in the Book of Hebrews, "Now may the God of peace, who brought again from the dead our Lord Jesus, *equip* you with everything good that you may do His will, working in you that which is pleasing in his sight, through Jesus Christ" (see Hebrews 13:20-21).

Christ Himself, who dwells in us by His Holy Spirit and mediates His life through us, prepares and makes us suitable to accomplish the particular, will He has for us. Thus, the New Testament theme, there is only *one foundation* that can be laid in our lives, Jesus Christ (see 1 Corinthians 3:11).

The five-fold ministers that Christ gave to the body must constantly be pointing to the all-sufficient Christ, to whom *each member* of the body is *directly* connected. Christ equips through these ministers by His Holy Spirit who dwells within them. Therefore, He speaks to each part of His body, the Church, through the various ministers and ministries who are filled and guided by the Holy Spirit (see John 14:12-18; Ephesians 5:18). In my book, *How Should We Then Live?* I express my belief that each title given in Ephesians 4:11 is actually a job description for each of these persons who are gifts of Christ and governmental leaders of the body of Christ, the Church.

Sadly, some ministers in the natural have blurred their supernatural assignment by trying to displace Christ as the Head. It is no wonder that in John 14 as Christ instructed His disciples concerning the ministry of the Holy Spirit, He emphasized the importance of keeping His commandments (see John 14:21). These equipping ministers as well as the rest of the body of Christ must walk in the commandment of love (see 1 John 4:7-11). Again, this is a supernatural walk (see 1 John 5:1-4, 14-18). The head does not tell the hand to tell the foot to walk; neither does the left hand tell the right hand to help it to lift an object. So every part must stay connected to the head and take full responsibility for its proper functioning. The role of the human equippers is to promote that connectedness with the rest of the body, the church.

The Word of God

Along with Jesus Christ as both the foundation and the builder, the written Word of God is fundamentally connected to establishing and laying foundations in a believer's life. Scripture in fact has an essential role in the equipping ministry as we discover in the well-known New Testament passage on the inspiration and authority of the Scriptures, *"All Scripture is given by inspiration of God, and is profitable for doctrine, for reproof, for correction, for instruction in righteousness, that the man of God may be complete, thoroughly equipped for every good work" (2 Timothy 3:16-17).*

The Word of God plays a vital part in equipping in several ways:

- **Teaching** – Creating a new worldview rooted in the new reality of the death, burial, and resurrection of Jesus Christ (Laying Foundations).

- **Reproof** – Confronting the sinfulness in our lives and putting us back in proper alignment (Restoring).

- **Correction** – Exposing false teaching and reestablishing the only foundation, Jesus Christ (Restoring).

- **Training in Righteousness** – Walking in the commandment of love, wholeness, and in devotion to God (Laying Foundations).

The goal or outcome of this work of God's Word is to make us complete so that we are *"equipped for every good work."* Meaning we are mature and prepared or enabled to do the work of ministry.

Just as we asked the question, what is the five-fold minister's relationship to Christ, the Head Equipper; we should ask, what is the five-fold minister's relationship to the inspired Word of God? When we examine the five gifted ones whom Christ gave to equip the saints for ministry in Ephesians 4:11 note that they have in common the different ways they implement the Word of God. The use of God's Word varies according to the particular equipper's function. These Spirit-filled five-fold ministers are analogous to the systems of the human body:

- The *apostles* are to the body of Christ, the Church, as the skeletal system which supports your human body and protects your internal organs.

- The *prophet's* message is meant to quicken and activate the saints into their Spiritual gifts for ministry, and deals with the immorality of the people as the immune system that defends your body against attacks by infectious microorganisms.

- The *evangelist* passionately, carries the gospel to the lost and sees lives directed to Christ for salvation, comparable to the digestive system which takes in food and changes it to new life.

- The *pastor* is to help feed and cleanse the body; similar to the circulatory system, that has the function of making sure that oxygen (life) reaches all cells of the body and removes waste.

- The *teacher* is to create a new world view rooted in the teaching of the Word of God line upon line, precept upon precept within the body of Christ as the brain and nervous system interprets information gathered through the senses initiates all body movement, stores information for later use, and controls thought and behavior.

Example the Incarnate Way

Human beings are the filters through which the Word of God incarnate and the written Word of God come to us. People are the embodiment of Christ and the written Word. The saying goes, "We are the only Bible many people will ever read."

In God's design, the means by which He affects people's lives are fallible *examples*. His ministry method is incarnation. He showed Himself in a Man (Jesus Christ). He continues to show Himself through man in whom He dwells through the Holy Spirit. A disciple is not above his or her teacher, but everyone when fully *taught* (matured) will be like their teacher *[my paraphrase]* (see Luke 6:40). Christian maturity does not result from the accumulation of head knowledge. Jesus believed that a teacher's role was to be an example in the disciple's life of what he or she was expected to learn.

Another way to laying foundations that are foundational to people becoming mature in Christ is disciple-making through association. During Timothy's long years of close association with Paul, he heard divine truth which God had revealed through Paul. Timothy was to take the divine truth he had learned from Paul and teach it to *other faithful men* with proven spiritual character and giftedness, who would in turn pass on those truths to another generation (see 2 Timothy 2:2).

Today we are raising a generation of young people who have little knowledge of God's Word (the Bible) or its contents. If they do have a salvation experience many have to go it alone, because churches do very little disciple-making of their converts. It's not long before Satan has stolen away what they did have. Not only those converts in the church; but also those in the workplace, family, friends, neighbors, and acquaintances. One possible reason for this terrible shortcoming is the heavy emphasis placed on denominational doctrine and denominational training; which in many cases has precedence over biblical doctrine and disciple-making training. The Word of God and its fundamental doctrines form the very life of the local church and everyday Christian living.

I believe the solution here has to be a long-term investment of *life into life* (one on one). Ninety percent of Christians have never had someone take them under their wing and make sure that the basic disciplines, doctrines, character qualities, or ministry issues have been instilled into their lives. This occurs when someone invests himself or herself in the life of another to guide them in the breadth and depth of the new life in Christ.

III. Preparation for Ministry (See Romans 9:23; Ephesians 4:12; Hebrews 10:5).

In relation to artistry and craftsmanship, "to equip" meant to work with the hands to produce something *useful* and *beautiful*. Ephesians 4:12 had a product in mind. The five-fold ministers of Ephesians 4:11 are to *"equip the saints for the work of ministry."*

The people are to find out what their aptitudes and abilities are for ministry as the appropriate five-fold minister exercises their gifts. This implies that particular training will be needed to prepare the people to exercise their ministry in the body of Christ, and to the world. Refining skills and practicing opportunities will be essential for a prepared ministry and must be proved.

The question may be asked, why do pastors attend seminary or Bible College and receive professional training? Is it so they can be set apart as a class (clergy) and then exercise their gifts over a passive (laity)? NO! The professional training is to be given away to the church so the people can be empowered to carry out the church's ministry. Pastors should be professionally equipped so they can give away their ministry. This is the biblical concept. This should not be problematic if we are Spirit-filled and Spirit-led children of God.

If it is true that all ministry is body ministry, then every area traditionally associated with pastoral ministry, with the possible exception of *preaching can be performed by duly Spiritually-gifted and called members of the body.* The pastor's role, therefore, is not to do the body's ministry, but to build teams of people to share the ministry in the different aspects of the pastor's giftedness. Though we share the ministry in the different aspects of the pastor's giftedness, we are reminded that we are to be a nation of priests, (See 1 Peter 2:9) not a nation of lay persons who are led by priests. Every believer is equally a priest before God. This means that no mediator stands between us and God other than our High Priest, Jesus Christ Himself.

We have direct and ready access to the Father. Being a priest also means that we are responsible for *bearing the witness* of Christ to others who need God's saving grace. Peter wrote that, as priests, our service to God is that of offering up spiritual sacrifices. These include the sacrifice of *praise* and *thanksgiving.* Only when Christ is truly Lord of our lives can He begin to place us into His *purpose.*

Personal Journal Notes

(Reflection & Response)

1. The most important thing that I learned from this chapter was:

2. The area that I need to work on the most is:

3. I can apply this lesson to my life by:

4. Closing Statement of Commitment

❧

Section V

Equipping: The Saints

Chapter 15

Equipping: The Body

In Chapter 12, I stated, that in God's eternal purpose, He had in mind that His Son should have a body to express His life. In other words that body would be the church, a new creation. God's eternal plan is a straight line. Theologians have distorted that plan by including sin as a part of it. Sin as in the case with Adam and Eve has always been external (outside); so if it's in the church it had to be brought in from the outside.

As a result of this distorted theology sin has been given a prominent position in the scheme of things that was never intended. For example in the church sin is given more prominence than righteousness. Much preaching is telling people what is wrong at the expense of not telling them what is right; and therefore millions go into eternity having never really heard the gospel truth.

The Church
The Church (the Body of Christ) is something which is beyond sin and has never been touched by sin. Listen to the apostle John, *"Whoever has been born of God does not sin, for His seed remains in him; and he cannot sin, because he has been born of God" (1 John 3:9).*

Much of what is preached on this point is filtered through a theology that puts limits on God. If His word says "does not sin" and if I say something else is true, then I'm not hearing or understanding God. I heard a preacher recently expounding on this very Scripture on the radio. As he read the passage no doubt from his own notes, he inserted the word *practice* in front of the word sin. However, we should never for a moment forget that greater is He that is in us, than he that is in the world. The Holy Spirit and the Word of God are given to keep us from falling.

Man's perspective is so different from God's perspective. The Bible tells us that, Christ's divine power has given to us (new creatures) all things that pertain to life and godliness, through the *knowledge of Him* who *called us* by glory and virtue (see 2 Peter 1:4). Above John speaks of *His seed* which remains in us. The apostle Peter speaks of exceedingly and precious promises made possible through the incarnate life of Christ in us through the Holy Spirit, who reside within (see John 14:15-17).

Verse 16 begins with "And." This means that until I get a handle on verse 15 which deals with loving the Lord and keeping His commandments, I cannot attain to verse 17. There are various reasons for not attaining. One is not having a loving and knowing relationship with Christ. Remember we said earlier, "knowing" denotes an intimate relationship out of which comes a birthing. Jesus said it frankly, *"Ye must be born again" (John 3:3) KJV.*

Later He said, *"But seek first the kingdom of God and His righteousness, and all these things shall be added unto you" (Matthew 6:33).* To comprehend what the Holy Spirit is saying to us here requires a renewed worldview. Christ is now our Source for everything. Rather than being preoccupied with material things which is the way of the world, our ambition should be to *seek first* God's *kingdom* and *His righteousness*, knowing that as we do so, He has pledged Himself with covenant faithfulness to respond and *all these things shall be added to you.* Paul adds, *"bodily exercise profits a little, but godliness is profitable for all things, having promise of life that now is and of that which is to come" (1 Timothy 4:8).*

Recognize that godliness is necessary to this life and to life eternal. We must be disciplined not only in body (upon which billions of dollars are spent each year to keep or improve), while so little care for the soul and spirit (what a shame in comparison). The salvation that God has intended for all men (and not to be tampered with theologically) He gives to those who believe and receive it. Those who believe not, who fail to appropriate the riches of God's grace (undeserved favor), will have an eternity to ponder their regrets (see 1 Timothy 4:10).

What I have expressed above is what God desires of us in reference to His purpose. Certainly Satan has his people to try and derail us mainly through distractions; but we can live this life of God by His Spirit and Word 24/7. The Word admonishes us to *"Walk in the Light as He is in the light" (I John 1:7).* The Bible declares, "God is light!"

Holy Spirit Conviction

Several biblical facts should be made at this point about the saint and sin. When we sin (make a mistake unintentionally, miss the mark), God gives us grace to confess it and He promises to be faithful and just to forgive us and the blood of Jesus washes it away. In that sense it is just as if we had not sinned. However, as stated earlier, to not confess, and seek forgiveness is of the devil for it can only happen in his territory (darkness). Those of us who truly belong to Christ will yield to the Spirit's conviction or be chastised of God, who promised that He chastises those He loves. God is not after you; but He is after sin and its source.

Those of us who are Christ's should have a zeal for righteousness, a zeal for the truth of His Word, and a zeal to live in appreciation of His grace and mercy toward us. And therefore live a life of worship and praise to the glory of God. We are in the world, but not of the world. We are supernatural! Now that's not an opinion, that's scriptural, and it requires a totally different worldview than the one we possessed before our rebirth.

How are we supernatural? Paul answers, *"For if when we were enemies we were reconciled to God through the death of His son, much more, having been reconciled, we shall be saved by His life" (Romans 5:10).*We are saved as we allow Him to manifest His life and His glory through us. In my loving everybody, it is Jesus Christ who loves through me; my teaching is His teaching through me by the Spirit. My life is His life through me. God sees only one of two men each time He looks at man or woman. He sees either Jesus or Adam. Behold the Man!

Therefore, every truly born again Christian is a minister of reconciliation. This ministry assigned by Christ allows Him to use us for His purpose and glory with the desire of reconciling all men back to God. It is not His will that any should perish.

Equipping the Body

Jesus spent His ministry showing His disciples how to bring kingdom power to bear on the works of the devil. Our ministry is His ministry. We cannot afford to work apart from the supernatural intervention and reality of the kingdom. Our assignment has never been about what we can do for Christ, but what He can do through us. That is the essence of the gospel, to do what Jesus did and that is to destroy the works of Satan.

Miracles, salvation, deliverance, revelation, prophecy, words of knowledge, the gifts of Christ, (the five-fold ministers), and Spiritual gifts are all normal elements of Christianity. To return the church's ministry back to its original mission requires a radical change in paradigm; which again requires a worldview change. For ministry to be returned to the people of God, we must have a bottom-up view of the local church. This is the organism (living) view of ministry, where ministry resides in the people, versus the church viewed as an institution, with a top down view of leadership. Let's contrast, a living organism view and the institutional view of the church. Notice the following characteristics of the church as a living organism:

- The organism (living) church defines itself from the bottom up as the whole people of God. This is the corporate *"a living sacrifice"* of Romans 12:1-2, a group of committed people of God who have personally *"presented their bodies"* to God.

- The biblical worldview causes us to shift our thinking for defining ministry from the institutional view of the ordained clergy to the organism view of body life.

- The ministry of the people of God cannot be an added attachment onto the root of ordained ministry; but ordained ministry must find its place within the people of God.

- Therefore, there is one ministry (body), the people's ministry that is derived from the one corporate "living sacrifice."

- The Holy Spirit is the Administrator of the living organism; He is quenched in the institutional church because His role is occupied by leadership at the top to whom the church itself is no longer the means to an end but is an end in itself.

The churches face a radical choice today of either sticking to the customs and traditions of men or see Holy Spirit led ministry, where members have particular roles to play according to their Spiritual giftedness within the body. I have stressed in the churches that I have been privileged to pastor the importance of the ministry of all believers. Because all truly born again members are parts of the body of Christ; they are in contact with the Head. This is so important; as the Head can use each of us to minister inside as well as engage in evangelism and social ministry outside of the four walls of the church.

Personal Journal Notes
(Reflection & Response)

1. The most important thing that I learned from this chapter was:

2. The area that I need to work on the most is:

3. I can apply this lesson to my life by:

4. Closing Statement of Commitment

CHAPTER 16

Equipping: The Local Church

The local church's ministry is more than simply winning and maturing people to Christ. It is also spreading the kingdom of God by working for the healing of people, families, communities, and relationships; by doing deeds of mercy and seeking justice. It is God's authority to bring in the blessedness of the kingdom through ordering lives, relationships, and institutions (see Isaiah 58).

Ministering to the Whole Man

For the past hundred years the local church has suffered a division; that has truly affected its mission. On one side are those who believe the Great Commission's charge to lead individuals to a saving relationship with Jesus Christ is the primary task of the church (see Mathew 28:18-20).

On the other side are those who point to the parable of the sheep and the goats (see Matthew 25:31-46). The return of the Lord will usher in a judgment, which will divide people. The judgment will be based on moral character, and the character is revealed by good deeds or the lack of them. Good works do not produce good character; good character produces good works. So this side stresses that the calling of the local church is to care for those who are poor and to seek justice.

Both sides are on the right track but neither has the whole picture. These selective portions of Scripture and interpretations of the church's mission have led to a one-sided Christianity. The apostle John challenges the church, *"My little children, let us not love in word or in tongue, but in deed and truth"* (see 1 John 3:18). Love is a verb, an action word. There's an old saying, "people would rather see a sermon, than to hear one any day." You can't very well tell somebody about the love of Jesus Christ if you don't have that love in your own heart. Remember, it's the love that draws people to Christ.

Unless the church combines both points social action, and evangelism; we simply have lip service. This means any ministry of this nature is void of the Holy Spirit's transforming power. Our good works show the genuineness of what we profess (see James 2: 15-16, 18). I know of a ministry who navigates the poorer communities with clipboards noting needed repairs such as broken down steps, windows, doors and other safety and security needs. With the permission of the occupants the team makes the necessary repairs at no cost to the occupants; while part of the team does repairs others do evangelism. Another ministry I learned of was a housewife who purchased or collected children's jackets from yard sales, clearance sales and donations; then during the winter months of school she would cruise neighborhood school bus stops, when she saw a child without a jacket she would jump out, open the trunk fit them up and move on to the next stop. A third ministry was a man who passes out Bible tracts and witnesses for the Lord in some places that the average Christian would not be caught in. All are Christians but none were sent or supported by their local church. I'm sure there are many such ministries in the local churches' membership everywhere. What an opportunity to put some meat into the church's discipleship training. I have found that this is a very good way to identify your potential ministry team leaders. I've often used this technique while helping congregations to establish holistic ministry.

A simple congregation survey denoting what individual Christians are already doing on their own will amaze the average pastor. Your missions check book balance will tell the story.

The Commands of Jesus

When Jesus sent out the Twelve on their first preaching mission, He told them, *"to preach the kingdom of God and to heal the sick" (Luke 9:2).* When Jesus sent out the Seventy, He told them, *"The kingdom of God has come near to you" (Luke 10:9).* That combination of preaching and healing was exactly what Jesus modeled, according to Matthew's critique of Jesus' ministry: *"Jesus went about all the cities and villages, teaching in the synagogues, preaching the gospel of the kingdom, and healing every sickness and every disease among the people" (Matthew 9:35).* This summary introduces the Commission He gave to His disciples. As Jesus prepared to leave His disciples, He charged them to carry on His mission in the world: *"As the Father has sent Me, so I send you" (John 20:21).*

Jesus' final instructions in the Great Commission (see Matthew 28:18-20) also point to word and deed. The church fulfills the basic command of making disciples in a two-fold manner:

- By baptizing those who accept Jesus Christ as their personal Savior, and

- By teaching them to obey everything that [Jesus has] commanded you (see v. 20).

Jesus commanded His disciples both to heal and to preach. If He combined *word* and *deed* and then commanded His followers to do the same, then the church dares not focus *only* on evangelism or *only* on social ministry.

The Gospel according to Jesus

If Jesus had defined the gospel only as the forgiveness of sins, then we could focus all our energy and resources on getting sinners to accept God's forgiveness through the blood of Jesus. Once they accept salvation and eternal life, they could continue refusing to change other parts of their lives. Instead, Jesus repeatedly said the gospel is the Good News of the kingdom (see Luke 4:43; 16:16).

The prophets told of the future Messiah who would usher in the messianic kingdom or reign of God. The kingdom would be characterized by renewed right relationships with God and neighbors, bringing forgiveness and justice especially for the poor (see Isaiah 9:1-7; 11:1-9; Jeremiah 31:31-34).

The fact that *faith* in Jesus was transforming the broken hearted, healing the crippled, the blind, the lame, the sick and the poor, was evidence that Jesus was the Messiah (see Matthew 11:4-5). Our sharing of the gospel is definitely not biblical unless our words and actions present the vertical and horizontal work of transformation as Jesus' produced.

Certainly there are numerous opportunities for such work of the church today. The changing economy, fuel and food prices, unemployment, and longevity has produced a myriad of spiritual and physical needs resulting in much despair and hopelessness for those without Christ in their lives. Church history points out that during the past one hundred years the church has been going through tremendous change and restoration. Unlike the changes that took place in the prior two centuries wherein an individual was used as the Spirit's change agent, today's change through restoration has been instituted by the Holy Spirit Himself mostly through groups large and small.

There are several beliefs concerning the Holy Spirit's presence and participation in the world and church today. These beliefs move from His coming on the Day of Pentecost and then returning to Heaven once the Bible was written, to His being Jesus' replacement here with the people of God after His ascension. These two theologies clash frequently in the local churches. Think about it one group is Holy Spirit filled (spiritual) and the other group is without the Spirit (non-spiritual).

A cursory examination of the Scriptures reveals that the Holy Spirit draws us then quickens our dead spirit in the regeneration process and takes up residence in our hearts. In fact we cannot possibly live a Christian life nor be the body of Christ without His constant presence. Jesus promised that He would be leaving, but He would send the Holy Spirit who would come and make His abode not with us as He was with His disciples; but the Holy Spirit (of Truth) would abide in us forever (see John 14:16-17). In verse 26 of this same chapter Jesus speaks of the Holy Spirit's teaching ministry, teaching us all things, and bringing to our remembrance those things He has told us. Also He speaks of the Holy Spirit's ministry of empowering us to witness (see John 15:26).

In the gospels Jesus repeatedly reminds us that He lived in total dependence on the Father incarnate in Him. Reading through His commandments we find that the same is expected of us. The promises that Christ left with and for us seem to all be preceded by His commandment of love to God and to our neighbor. He promised that the coming of the Spirit was dependent upon His leaving to return to the right hand of the Father, where He is today.

Jesus continues to tell us what is expected of the Holy Spirit (vv. 8-12). He points to the *supernatural* revelation of all truth by which God has revealed Himself in Christ (vv. 13-15). In (vv. 16-19) Jesus referring to His ascension "you will not see Me" and the coming of the Holy Spirit "you will see Me," emphatically claiming that the Spirit and He are One (see Romans 8:9; Philippians 1:19; 1 Peter 1:11; Revelation 19:10). *Christ dwells in believers through the Holy Spirit;* in that sense they see Him.

Again we turn to church history. There we read of the Azusa Street revivals in Los Angeles, California in 1906. It seems that the Holy Spirit was returning fully to the church after an absence of about 1100 years; while the Roman Catholic Church was the main depository of Christianity. Several features of this revival would make even the unsaved realize that it had to be a mighty move of God:

- First of all the Holy Spirit used a black preacher, William Seymour as His change agent.

- Secondly, it lasted some three years, next it was multiracial, and finally people came from around the country and the world similar to the Day of Pentecost.

- People returned to their home communities and churches baptized in the Holy Spirit and speaking with other tongues.

- This movement began in 1906 is still in progress more than 100 years later.

- In fact, many studies today reflect that the fastest growing churches today can trace their beginnings back to someone who attended that Pentecostal revival.

In my personal research I have found that many notable church personalities of that day refused to even go and investigate what was going on. For whatever reason or reasons the church continues to be divided today into what I call the spiritual and non-spiritual. I read the story of the conflict, one evangelist from my home State of North Carolina; who had traveled for days on a train with a one-way ticket just to find out that the change agent the Holy Spirit was using was a black man. The article stated that he wandered around for several days dealing with the problem but eventually decided to go in. I praised God as I read this article because of the fact that this evangelist undoubtedly came to himself and acknowledged that he was a new creature in Christ Jesus (see 2 Corinthians 5:17) eventually overcoming his hang-ups undoubtedly through the Holy Spirit's leading. Praise God! I attended the Heritage Bible College which is located in the county area that this preacher returned to. I felt and became acquainted with his influence even before I heard his name.

Spirit-Filled Christians

The "koinania" (love and unity) of chapter 4 of Acts gives way to the Ananias and Sapphira of chapter 5:1-11. In chapter 6 of the Book of Acts a problem arose in the church which the apostles solved by creating a division of ministries to prevent a division of the people. The "Hellenists" (Jews from the Diaspora) believed their widows were not receiving a fair share of the food the church provided for their care (see Acts 6:1-6). Widows in deed continue to be a special consideration of the church today (I Timothy 5:1-6).

Much confusion over this passage of Scripture has risen over the centuries. One that I have become well acquainted with in my years as pastor; that these seven men were deacons. Simply put there is nothing to indicate that this group of seven men appointed were deacons, yet many institutional churches use this Scripture in reference to that church office (see I Timothy 3:8-13). Just as when we discussed the pastor in the top down example, we experience the same problems with this office. The decision-making process excludes the people and in some instances even the pastor. This leads to passive congregations who believe that only the church leaders are required to be Spirit-filled.

My studies of this passage have revealed that the Greek term "diakonias" is actually translated "servant." From my personal experience "full of the Holy Ghost" would be saying *be sure, be very sure* that these individuals are filled with the Holy Ghost. The church's mission demands organization and delegation. Indicated here also is the fact that in the church there are those who are not Spirit-filled. Therefore, it would do us well to realize that "diakonias" refers to all of us, as we are all servants, those who have reached the "walk in the Spirit" of Romans 8:1. This translates to all choir members, ushers, and all other Christian workers from the pulpit to the door in the local church. Back in Acts 2:4 we see that *all,* of the apostles and the 120 were filled with the Holy Spirit. In contrast to the baptism of the Holy Spirit, which is the one-time act by which God places believers into His body (see 1 Corinthians 12:13), the filling is a repeated reality of *Spirit-controlled* behavior that Christ, the Head of the Church, commands *all* believers to maintain (see Ephesians 5:18).

Peter and many others in Acts 2 were filled with the Spirit again, for example (see Acts 4:8, 31; 6:5; 7:55) their destinies were guided by the Spirit and they boldly spoke the Word of God; not only boldness, but the fullness of the Spirit motivated their life-ministries and affected all areas of their lives.

Christian Accountability

Many of the commands in the Bible are not popular today. One such command is found in the Book of Hebrews, *"Obey those who rule over you, and be submissive, for they watch out for your souls, as those who must give account. Let them do so with joy and not with grief, for that would be unprofitable for them" (Hebrews 13:17).*

Here just as noted of other commands in prior chapters is one of those commands; that is impossible to obey in your own natural strength. Unless one is being transformed from a selfish and self-driven individual to one who lives for and surrenders control of one's life to God, the practice of accountability for life choices and behavior is futile. All Christians are responsible for integrating biblical beliefs and principles into their lives and their church is to hold them accountable.

The most common approach for accountability among churches is through Christian small groups. This group is an intentional "face-to-face" encounter of no more than twelve people who meet on a regular basis with the purpose of growing in the knowledge and likeness of our Lord and Savior, Jesus Christ.

Coming to know Christ means being introduced into the body of Christ; none remain isolated individuals. God creatively recognizes both individual and group by introducing the concept of the individual in the group. In balance, both the individual's relationship to God and the corporate relationship to God are developed in the overall plan. The individual is not lost or engulfed by his or her solidarity with the group. It is the group that brings self-awareness and a sense of identity to the individual. I am of the group but uniquely my own person.

Neither the church nor any of its small groups are collective, but are corporate. The individuals are not identical but are members of the body of Christ (see 1 Corinthians 12:20-30). Other goals of the small group include:

- Prepare and aid the individual in his or her integration into the full body life of the church.

- It requires constant commitment to interdependence and to keep this value before the group.

- Assist the individual in developing their spiritual gift.

- Help the individual in developing their daily spiritual disciplines.

- Take Jesus' life as your model for suffering and obedience.

- Obey church leadership.

- Be focused on others.

The night is far spent, the day is at hand. Therefore let us cast off the works of darkness, and let us put on the armor of light. Let us walk properly, as in the day, not in revelry, and drunkenness, nor in lewdness and lust, not in strife and envy. But put on the Lord Jesus Christ, and make no provision for the flesh, to fulfill its lusts" (Romans 13:12-14).

The prudent see danger and take refuge, but the simple keep going and suffer for it (Proverbs 27:12).

Anything that causes us to lose our thirst for righteousness, anything that hinders us in our pursuit, those things we must cast off. Is there a TV program, website, or certain kind of thought, person, or situation you need to flee? Are you willing to give it up for Christ? Are you willing to run? Wisdom says, "Ask a couple of friends to keep a check on you.

Personal Journal Notes

(Reflection & Response)

1. The most important thing that I learned from this chapter was:

2. The area that I need to work on the most is:

3. I can apply this lesson to my life by:

4. Closing Statement of Commitment

CHAPTER 17

Equipping: The Saints through the Truth

he Word of God commands that we not be conformed to this world; but we are to be transformed by the renewing of our minds. This can happen only through yielding ourselves to the teaching of the Word of God. The Word of God is the Spirit's instrument of transformation. The Word of God is truth; and it is the truth that transforms.

God's Word is Foundational

Once you learn that you can stand on God's Word as the foundation for your life, the Word must be given first place in all areas of your life applications: thoughts, decisions, and actions. Rather than looking at the Word through your circumstances and situations which make them loom much larger than they actually are; see your situations and circumstances through the Word of God. What are the truths of life's situations and circumstances? We'll realize the answer to that question more and more with each passing year that we walk with the Lord who is Truth.

While renewing your mind through the Spirit and His Word, you will receive a clear understanding of who you are and whose you are in Him, then your faith in Him and the assurance of your calling as a saint grows deeper and more powerful with the passing of time. Not only that, we will know God's will for our lives as He reveals it to us through His Spirit and His Word.

One of the all-time promises for New Testament saints as well as it was for Old Testament saints was given to Joshua by the Lord Himself. He told Joshua,

"This Book of the Law shall not depart from your mouth, but you shall meditate in it day and night, that you may observe to do according to all that is written in it. For then you will make your way prosperous, and then you will have good success" (Joshua 1:8).

Joshua is told that the way he and Israel would take the Promised Land was through meditation of God's Word "day and night" in His Law, in this case, the first five books of the Bible written by Moses. His obedience yielded great success.

I've heard Christians admit that they are too busy to study the Bible; so they certainly have nothing stored on which to meditate. Isn't it amazing that Joshua, the highest ranking, and busiest man in Israel after Moses, now promoted to Commander in Chief of the Lord's army would receive such an order from his Commander?

He had great success because he simply obeyed. Checking his track record, it was all in a day's work. God's promises carry the same weight for New Testament saints today. Keeping our minds filled with the Word of God leaves no room for Satan's suggestions. We will always have a Word to apply to life's circumstances.

Study to show thyself Approved

Jesus said to him, "I am the way, the truth, and the life; no one comes to the Father, except through Me" (John 14:6).

We see from this Scripture verse that Jesus is the Truth, the Living Word. Jesus is the substance of Truth. Therefore, as we read, study, and meditate on the Word of God; we are literally partaking of Jesus, the Truth, and becoming like Him. Behold the Man!

Be diligent to present yourself approved to God, a worker who does not need to be ashamed, rightly dividing the word of truth (2 Timothy 2:1). We see the antithesis in this verse, if we can rightly divide the Word of truth, then we can certainly wrongly divide the Word of truth. Many times we take the Word of God out of context by just reading a couple of verses, then passing on our assumptions, never considering what the remainder of the chapter has to say. The wider problem here is the tragedy of the church fragmented through this practice. I personally know of a church that was founded on the practice of praise through music. The preaching and teaching of God's truth has been given a lower priority. The Sunday morning crowd is very well entertained. Satan is pleased!

Study, study, and study! The devil cannot compete with truth. He can't affect your life unless he can pull you away from the Word of God or distort and pervert it. To get that done he will deceive you, distract you, and seduce you to steal the Word from your heart. How easy is this for him to do? It could prove very damaging for young converts. I heard a very popular radio talk-show host boast, "don't read the newspapers, save your money and listen to me." It may not be said this way in our local churches, however in many of them the teaching of doctrinal truth is not a priority; and therefore the people are left to fend for themselves.

Saints must be taught

The Christian life is not as hard as so many people in the church claim it to be. If we abide in the Word, it will transform us so that we will know God's perfect will. That's the promise of God's Word (see Romans 12:1-2). Notice also, *"to be spiritually minded is life and peace" (Romans 8:6)*. Being spiritually minded is being Word minded (see John 6:63).The seed is God's Word. The ground is our hearts. And the fruit is that we all long for holiness.

The saints of God must be taught, said another way, God's Word has to be planted in our hearts. Jesus confirmed this through a parable, *"The kingdom of God is as if a man should scatter seed on the ground; and should sleep by night and rise by day, and the seed should sprout and grow, he himself does not know how. The earth yields crops by itself; first the blade, then the head, after that the full grain in the head. But when the grain ripens, immediately he puts in the sickle, because the harvest has come" (Mark 4:26-29)*.

In the parable, to illustrate truths about how God's Word works, Jesus used an example of seed, time, and harvest, which was widely understood by the people, being an agrarian society:

- He taught that God's Word has to be planted like a seed into our hearts; just as a seed doesn't release its life within until it is planted into the ground, God's Word will not work for us until we get it in our hearts. Carrying the Bible around on the dashboard, in our hands, or in our heads is not enough; we must commit God's Word to our hearts, and act upon it

- The man in Jesus' parable, who sowed the seed, slept and arose day in and day out. It takes time for a seed to germinate. You can't plant a seed today and expect to see it pop up through the soil tomorrow. Yet, just because there's nothing visible above the ground doesn't mean the seed is not growing. You must have faith that the seed will do what it is designed by God, its Creator, to do; and that is to produce its fruit in its season. The Word of God works the same way. When we meditate on God's Word, we see the growth in its time. During the wait, we learn patience.

For reinforcement we have the promise of John 15:7-8 where Jesus says, *"If you abide in Me, and my words abide in you, you will ask what you desire, and it shall be done for you. By this My Father is glorified, that you bear much fruit; so you will be My disciples.*

Jesus gave one of the most important truths of the parable. He said, *"The seed should sprout and grow up, he himself does not know how."* No one knows how a seed works. Man, with all of his scientific ingenuity and understanding has not been able to unlock the miracle of the seed. Man can produce an artificial seed that looks like, taste like a real seed, and even have the exact chemical makeup as a seed, but if it's planted, it will not sprout and grow because there is no life in it.

We've all heard and read of seeds buried in containers with people over thousands of years. When the seeds were removed and planted in the ground, after all of those years in the tomb, sprang to life; and yielded a harvest. We don't know how but it's obvious from observation, the seed has the power or life within to reproduce itself; if it is planted in good ground.

I don't understand how the seed of God's Word planted in our hearts works either; but again from observation, that Seed (Word) has the power or life within to reproduce itself; if it is planted in good ground (heart). Like the artificial seed above, opinions and words read from some other sources will not sprout and grow. Only the Word of God, His truth has that power and life. I don't understand it all but I do know that it works. Through the years I have experienced and enjoyed the supernatural life that God's Word imparts. Please try it; get into the Word and let it truly get into your heart. Oh! What a change in my life has been wrought since the truth of God's Word has been planted in my heart. Praise God!

I pray that you see how futile much of what is used in the local church for Christian education really is. Jesus was the only person who gave the world a perfect look at God living through a person. Though we will never be the express image of God in the way Jesus was, as the saints of God, we have the seed within our hearts to express Him in a much greater way than we do. In order to do that, we must change. Growth always requires change. So, if we're not experiencing any growth in our lives, it may be because of lean sowing of the Word in our hearts. Remember, we reap what we sow.

Too many Christians live far below their potential because they have been taught that God and Jesus are way up there in heaven, and Christians are way down here in this old dirty, sinful world. They claim that "saints aren't really saints." They are filthy, unworthy worms in the sight of God. They are "sinners saved by grace," just living "one day at a time." What they mean is that the blood of Jesus just barely allows them to slip into heaven when they die.

But that's not what the Bible says. It says, *"And has raised us up together, and made us sit together in the heavenly places in Christ Jesus" (Ephesians 2:6).* The believer is said to be *in Christ.* Christ is said to be "in the heavenly places." Therefore, the believer is in the heavenly realm of experience with Christ. True, the believer physically lives on earth, but spiritually he or she has already been placed "in the heavens." The believer is in both realms, belonging to two worlds. He or she has two addresses: *in Your Town* and *in Christ.* He or she maintains two relationships: one to earth and one to heaven (see Hebrews 3:1; 1 Peter 2:11).

Our salvation, resurrection, and exaltation, are accomplished facts. In the Word "together" or "with Him," a profound truth is unfolded. It is said that believers are already raised from the dead *with Christ* and already seated *with Christ* at the right hand of God. The words "quickened," "raised," and "made to sit" express what God has already done for His children in Christ. Christ has already died and been raised and exalted to live in heaven with God forever. God sees all things as they really are. Therefore, He sees believers as having *already* been raised and exalted to live eternally with Him, all because He sees them *in Christ Jesus.* He sees their faith and *counts* them as being in Christ. *"But if the Spirit of Him who raised Jesus from the dead dwells in you, He who raised up Christ from the dead will also give life to your mortal bodies through His Spirit who dwells in you" (Romans 8:11).*

When you know the Truth and your heart is well saturated with it; when the greatest physicians and hospitals say, "I'm sorry, we've done all we can do, nothing else can be done for them," you can say, "Let me pray the prayer of faith and they shall recover." You can solve every problem in your marriage and in your children's lives. And you can lead people to Christ and get them delivered also.

The problem with the Christian and the local church is no longer lack of leadership, education, or money, the neighborhood you come from, your personality or whatever. Now your *problem is a lack of truth!* Ignorance of what God's Word really says about you, the situation you are facing, and the world around you. You can get the truth you need by getting into the Word of God, believing it, meditating on it, and living it by faith; which is activated by love.

Personal Journal Notes
(Reflection & Response)

1. The most important thing that I learned from this chapter was:

2. The area that I need to work on the most is:

3. I can apply this lesson to my life by:

4. Closing Statement of Commitment

CHAPTER 18

Equipping: The Saints through Spiritual Gifts

M any churches fail to grasp the awesome concept designed by God for His church to influence the world. The apostle Paul outlines it for us in the "operating manual" for the new body of Christ on earth, the church, in Ephesians 4. *"Grace was given to each of us according to the measure of Christ's gift" (v.7).* This grace is a God-given capacity for service that we have received as Christians. This grace is resident in the Holy Spirit, who indwells us and is given without exception to all true Christians.

Upon conversion in the early church new converts were taught in the apostles' doctrine, worship, prayer, fellowship and Christ's life that the Holy Spirit imparted to them; but also equipped them with a Spiritual gifts; which he or she was then responsible to exercise for the "common good" of the body (see 1 Corinthians 12:7; and 1 Peter 4:10). In each place that the gifts of the Spirit are described in Scripture, the emphasis is upon the fact that each true Christian has at least one. Your destiny is determined by the degree to which you use the gift (s) God has given you.

I have emphasized "true Christian," lest we forget that Satan has his counterfeits and then there are those who are naturally talented. Both of these can tremendously hinder the Holy Spirit's work through those who are gifted by Him for service.

New Testament Fellowship (Koinionia)

One of the essentials for an authentic church as seen in the Book of Acts is "fellowship." Certainly I am not speaking of doughnuts and coffee; though each of us no doubt has enjoyed immensely that activity. The Greek term for fellowship is "koinonia." This koinonia is the New Testament kind of fellowship missing in too many churches today. I might add it cannot be attained without the Holy Spirit.

The New Testament lays heavy emphasis on the need for Christians to know each other, closely, and intimately enough to be able to *"love one another" (John 13:34) "bear one another's burdens" (Galatians 6:2) "confess faults one to another" (James 5:16) – encourage, exhort, and admonish one another, and minister to one another with the Word of God and prayer.* This is possible only among Spirit-filled Christians.

There are more than fifty *"one another"* Scriptures in the New Testament, and they call us to a special kind of life (konionia). These statements you'll find are commands of ministries in the body of Christ and are very important to God, since He speaks of them so frequently in His Word. Certainly a careful study and application of each would revitalize the life of the individual Christian and focus the body of Christ.

In many churches, there exists some expression of koinonia life taking place in private gatherings of Christians, usually in someone's home. However, I'm sad to report they are often misunderstood and short-lived because as soon as the leadership gets wind of it, these Christians are accused of trying to divide the church. In most cases the group is left with a choice of disbanding or leaving the church.

Authentic koinonia life doesn't threaten the *unity* of the church; the fact of the matter is, it should be the goal of every church. In the early church the observation of this concern for each other, and the way they shared their lives in the body of Christ, prompted a pagan writer to remark: "How these Christians love one another!" We can glean from the Book of Acts that it was the combination of *kerygma* (proclamation), *diadache* (teaching), and *koinonia* (love/ fellowship) that made the church's witness so powerful and effective. It was in this setting that the Scriptures says, *"And the Lord added to the church daily those who were being saved" (Acts 2:47).*

I interjected this explanation on the koinonia life because it is not only required for healthy church life, but it also provides a rich environment for the Spiritual gifts to operate effectively.

Spiritual Gifts and Ministry (Exercise)

Now, let's use our Bibles and find out what is taught about spiritual gifts:

1. What does "the body of Christ mean?" The church – it is the principal metaphor used to understand spiritual gifts (see Ephesians 1:20-23; Colossians 1:15-18).

What does the above Scriptures say about the "body of Christ"?:

_____

_____

_____

2. What system did God choose for the internal organization of the body of Christ?

It is not: A dictatorship (one person rules the body)

It is not: A democracy (all members rule)

It is: An *organism* with Christ as the Head and with each member functioning therein with a spiritual gift.

What does I Corinthians 12:12-27 have to say?

_____

_____

_____

3. What is a spiritual gift? A spiritual gift is a special attribute given by the Holy Spirit to *every* member of the body." The Greek is *"charismata"* meaning "grace gifts".

4. How many people have spiritual gifts? All true Christians have one or more gifts.

What does I Peter 4:10 and I Corinthians 12:7 have to say?

_____

_____

_____

5. Why do you need to know about spiritual gifts?

They will benefit: You in your own spiritual life and enable you for serving others.

They will benefit: The entire church (a new vitality enters the church's life).

They will help you to know God's will for your life.

What does Romans 12:1-6 have to say?

_____

_____

_____

6. Three of the most important goals in your Christian life should be:

Discover your spiritual gift (s)

Develop your spiritual gift (s)

Use your spiritual gifts (s)

7. Why does discover come before develop? The gift has already been given to you by grace; gifts are not received, nor achieved.

What does I Corinthians 12:7-11, 18 have to say?

_____

_____

_____

What happens if I decide not to discover, develop and use my spiritual gift (s)? I will have to answer to God, for I am a steward of the gifts He's given me.

What does 1Peter 4:10 have to say?

_____

_____

_____

What does Matthew 25:14-30 have to add?

_____

_____

_____

8. All right, suppose everyone in our church decides to discover, develop, and use their spiritual gift (s)? What will happen?

(1) Each member will *know* his or her spiritual job description.

(2) All members will be able to work together in love, harmony, and avoid envy, strife, pride, and false humility (see Romans 12:3).

_____

_____

_____

(3) The whole body will mature (see Ephesians 4:11-14).

_____

_____

_____

(4) The church will grow (see Ephesians 4:12, 16).

_____

_____

_____

(5) And, God will be glorified (see I Peter 4:10-11).

_____

_____

_____

Spiritual Gifts (I Corinthians 12:1-10)

In our study thus far, we should by now realize that Spiritual gifts are not God bestowing to His people something outside of Himself. Spiritual gifts are God Himself in us energizing our souls, imparting revelation to our renewed minds, infusing His power in our wills, our affections, and working His gracious purpose through us.

The apostle Paul in comparing the church to the human body shows how the wide diversity of gifts assures *unity* in the church. As you read take note of the italicized words:

Now there are varieties of gifts, but *the same Spirit.* And there are varieties of ministries, and *the same Lord.* And there are varieties of effects, but *the same God who works all things in all persons.* But to each one is given *the manifestation of the Spirit* for the common good. For to one is given the word of wisdom *through the Spirit,* and to another the word of knowledge *through the same Spirit;* to another faith *by the same Spirit,* and to another gifts of healing *by the Spirit,* and to another the effecting of miracles, and to another prophecy, and to another the discerning of spirits, to another various tongues, and to another the interpretation of tongues. But *one and the same Spirit works all these things, distributing to each one individually just as He wills (see vv.4-11).*

We will find additional Spiritual gifts in Romans 12; and some variations in other parts of the New Testament. The church desperately needs this infusion of the supernatural power and activity of God into its life and ministry. Like the members of the human body, the gifts are the members of the church body. Each member is important and plays a vital role in the proper functioning of the whole. Knowing the truth about the spiritual gifts, their availability and understanding how they function is essential if the local church is to ever to get on task as one.

The Holy Spirit left nothing for the church to figure out concerning Spiritual gifts. He gave the apostle Paul the list and description of the gifts in 1 Corinthians 12 and you'll notice He explains their operations in Chapter 14. The wisdom of God tells us that before we can operate or even get into the operations of the gifts, we must navigate chapter 13 (the love lesson). In the natural all the above are impossible for us; but through Christ we can do all things. Behold the Man!

As with the five gifts of Ephesians 4:11, apostles, prophets, evangelists, pastors, and teachers were given to the body of Christ by Christ, Himself; so these gifts are given to the local church by the Holy Spirit. In both cases, their very name denotes the individual's job description. Certainly, if the church leadership would humbly submit themselves to the truth of God's Word and to the Holy Spirit's leading, division, envy, jealousy and all other works of the flesh (See Galatians 5:19-20) that seems so accepted as a normal expectancy of church today would be eliminated. My prayer for the local church is that it moves on to its true expectancy in (vv. 21-22), the fruit of the Spirit (Christ likeness).

God's Secret

In the Epistle to the Ephesians, the apostle declared that God's "secret" in planning the church is no longer hidden; now the *mystery* is known. He has designed the church to administer Christ's fullness everywhere, ministering as a living body spreading over the Earth and penetrating "the heavens." God's "manifold wisdom" ("varied" in His people) now demonstrates His glory in the church *(His purpose),* (see 3:10-11), a manifestation that will eventually show up in the individual believer's strengthening (3:14-20), maturing *(speaking the truth in love, may grow up in all things into Him who is the Head Christ)* (see 4:15-16), confrontation and victory *(put on the whole armor of God),* (6:10-20). A disciple, equipped to do the work of ministry.

Simply put, the end product is one living the way God wants us to live, godly! Here in Ephesians, godliness is exhorted in terms of behavior, motivating dynamic, and example. Godly behavior is modeled after God Himself, especially as He has revealed Himself in His fullness in Jesus Christ. Behold the Man!

Personal Journal Notes

(Reflection & Response)

1. The most important thing that I learned from this chapter was:

2. The area that I need to work on the most is:

3. I can apply this lesson to my life by:

4. Closing Statement of Commitment